To Susie –

Go Pack Go!

Fuzzy

Thurston

63

6 x World Champion

I see skies of blue and clouds of white

The bright blessed day, the dark sacred night

And I think to myself, what a wonderful world.......

-Louis Armstrong

From Louis Armstrong's, "What A Wonderful World"

The title of this book was borrowed from the Louis Armstrong jazz classic and was chosen not only because it is one of Fuzzy Thurston's favorite songs, but more importantly as it represents Fuzzy Thurston's view of life despite the many obstacles and hardships he has faced.

WHAT A WONDERFUL WORLD

FUZZY THURSTON

A STORY OF PERSONAL TRIUMPH

Fuzzy & Sue Thurston
with Bill Wenzel

Photo Editing & Book Design By
Douglas T. Golner

Contributions by Chris Havel

Project Director
Jennifer Smith

Photography featured from the Vernon Biever collection
& the Thurstons' personal archives.

Published By Fuzzy Thurston and Bill Wenzel

Published in the United States

Photos appearing on pages 163,163,168 taken by
Randy Peterson, Countryside Photographers, Seymour Wisconsin

Other photos appear courtesy of Fuzzy and Sue Thurston

Lines from “Wonderful World" written by George Weiss, Bob Thiele

Book editing by: Andrew Peterson

ISBN-13: 978-0-9788941-0-8

Printed in the United States Of America

First Edition

fuzzybook.com

To my wife, Sue

My best friend and love of my life for 50 years

To my children Mark, Griff and Tori

Being your father is my greatest victory

And my grandkids Olivia, Freddy and Joey

You bring me great joy

To Packers fans everywhere

I love each and every one of you

Table of Contents

FOREWORD

It is no secret that I have always held my offensive linemen in high regard.

All eyes might be on the quarterback, but anyone that knows football knows it all starts with the guys up front. Frank Winters and Marco Rivera and Mike Flanagan and Mark Tauscher - I could go on and on and name every lineman I ever played with - because they are that special to me.

I don't win one Most Valuable Player award without them, let alone three MVPs, and the Green Bay Packers don't win Super Bowl XXXI or get to Super Bowl XXXII without them, either.

That is why it is a privilege and an honor to write this forward for one of my all-time favorites, and one of everyone's all-time favorites, Fred "Fuzzy" Thurston.

When I hear the name Fuzzy, and there's only one Fuzzy, I immediately think about the great Packers sweep. I can close my eyes and picture Thurston and (Jerry) Kramer pulling out to throw the lead blocks for Paul Hornung or Jim Taylor.

It was a thing of beauty, and Fuzzy was right in the heart of it.

The first time I met Fuzzy and shook his hand I thought, "Man, he doesn't know how strong he is." I also thought, "This is a man that loves the Packers as much as any fan or former player - or in his case both - possibly could."

Fuzzy stayed in Green Bay and opened a bar not because he could capitalize on his fame, but because he loves the Packers that much. He is the glue that keeps all those great players from the Lombardi Era together.

When they return for the alumni game each year there's never a question about where they're going to meet. It's a given that it's at Fuzzy's place. It's a homecoming, sort of like high school or college but on a much grander scale, and Fuzzy's is home.

If Bart Starr was the brilliant mind behind that team, and Paul Hornung and Jim Taylor were the heart, then Fuzzy and that offensive line was its soul.

The Packers have such a great tradition and that still means a lot. Whenever you hear or read about Green Bay, it's always something about, "the frozen tundra of Lambeau Field," or something about "Titletown, USA," or Vince Lombardi, or Bart Starr, or Ray Nitschke, or Paul Hornung, or Fuzzy Thurston, or something about those great teams from the sixties.

I have always loved football, so even when I was a kid I already knew something about the Green Bay Packers. When I was in fifth grade I did a book report on Paul Hornung. I probably got an A on it. I was always good at book reports. When I met Hornung I told him that, and he seemed to be impressed.

It was the same with Fuzzy.

When we started winning and going to the playoffs for the first time in what must have seemed like forever to Packers fans, Mike (Holmgren) occasionally would ask former Packers greats to come in and visit with us.

I'll always remember the excitement and enthusiasm all those players showed, and Fuzzy was right at the top of the list. He is so emotional, and he has such a great heart, that you can't help but be touched by that. He is also sincere and genuine, and he is proof that it's OK to be sensitive even if you're a rough and tough football player.

Fuzzy might be the biggest Packers fan in the world, which is saying a lot because we've got fans all over the country, people who used to live in Wisconsin and moved away but still follow the team with a passion. There are others who fell in love with the team during the Lombardi years and stuck by the team.

No matter where we play we have fans at the game, and I mean a lot of fans. It's like that in Detroit, and Minnesota, and a lot of places. The type of greeting we get before games, shoot, some teams would like to get that after a big win. That's what is so great.

And it's not just the fans that are passionate. Some of the older players from the 1996 Super Bowl (XXXI) team were just as emotional. Sean Jones, our defensive end that played opposite Reggie White, had played for the Raiders and the Oilers. I remember him telling me that he'd never seen anything like what the Packers have right here.

Jones said, "What people outside Green Bay don't understand is that for us to be validated as a great team we've first got to prove our greatness to the Willie Woods, the Willie Davises, the Bart Starrs, the Fuzzy Thurstons, all those great old players. I am convinced that the Ray Nitschkes and the Jerry Kramers and those guys probably don't think we could have played with them."

I never mind that kind of pressure. We do have a legacy to live up to and that's exciting. We are part of something that is bigger than the moment. A few weeks after the '96 Super Bowl I talked with Bart Starr and he told me he was so excited for the Packers that he still could hardly sleep. Now that's something. Here's Bart Starr, one of the greatest quarterbacks of all time, a Hall of Fame quarterback who won just about all there is to win in the 1960s, and he's excited as a schoolboy after we won the Super Bowl. That's what this team means to not only the community and the state but also to the old Packers. They want us to do well because they still feel they're part of the team, and Fuzzy wants us to do well because he feels like he's part of the team, which he is.

That makes me feel proud.

** BRETT FAVRE

Prologue

We all have a few defining moments in our life, moments in time where something happens that changes our life forever. I had one of those moments in 1986 when I met Fuzzy Thurston. My life has not been the same since. At first, I was thrilled just to meet a former Packers great from the Lombardi era, one of my boyhood idols growing up as a Packers fan in Chicago. Twenty years later, I rarely think of Fuzzy as a star football player. I think of him as a close personal friend, a good buddy. Today, we also enjoy a great relationship as business partners.

This is not a football story. Rather, it is a story about a great man that just happened to play pro football. Former Denver Broncos Head Coach Dan Reeves once said, "You can measure a man's character by the way he treats an individual that can do nothing for him." Fuzzy Thurston is a man of great character. Fuzzy always has a kind word, a smile and an autograph, if requested, for friends and strangers alike. He makes time for everyone.

Some of my best memories of Fuzzy are the conversations we had at Shenanigans during the cold winter months of the late 1980's. I would drive up from Chicago, where I was living, and we would talk for hours. Sometimes we were the only two people in the bar. I would listen to Fuzzy talk about the good old days – Lombardi, his teammates, anything Packers. Mostly, I wanted to know what it was like to live in Green Bay when the Packers won the Super Bowl. I needed to know because I wasn't sure I would ever experience that feeling. I moved to Green Bay in 1993. I feel fortunate to have had the opportunity to live in Green Bay and share the experience of the 1996 Super Bowl Championship with Fuzzy Thurston. Those are memories I will never forget.

With Fuzzy, the glass isn't half-full, it's overflowing. Fuzzy is ALWAYS in a good mood, no matter what the circumstances. And it's contagious – Fuzzy makes everyone with him feel better. Because of throat cancer, Fuzzy can't speak very well. I really wish I could have met him before the surgery, just to hear what he sounded like. People tell me that he was the life of the party. In reality, Fuzzy doesn't need to speak with his voice. His attitude, mannerisms, smile and sheer presence speak volumes. He is still the life of the party!

Fuzzy Thurston has had a rewarding, but very tough life. As you will read in this book, Fuzzy has overcome the loss of his father as a young child, poverty, cancer and bankruptcy. He overcame insurmountable odds to earn a basketball scholarship to Valparaiso University and later play on the great Packers championship teams of the 1960's. His life story is a great example of what a person can accomplish with a positive attitude, a great work ethic and the support of loved ones.

In recent years, great Packers "fans" have been inducted into the Packers Hall of Fame. Fuzzy Thurston is already a member of the Packers Hall of Fame as a player, but he could also be inducted as a fan. His love for the team and the organization is second to none. Fuzzy loves to sing karaoke on Packers weekends. He ends each performance with the words "God bless the Green Bay Packers," to the delight of the crowd.

Fuzzy Thurston has been serving Packers fans on and off the field since 1959. Fuzzy was an integral part of the Packers teams that won 5 World Championships and 2 Super Bowl Championships. He owns Fuzzy's 63 Bar in Green Bay, where former players and fans can meet. He participates in numerous golf outings and events to raise money for charity. He has basically lived in Wisconsin since birth and in the Green Bay area his entire adult life. If there were a Mr. Packer, it would be Fuzzy Thurston. No player in Packers history has had such a great love for the team and its fans. No player in Packers history is more loved than Fred "Fuzzy" Thurston.

I hope you enjoy and are inspired by his life story.

Bill Wenzel

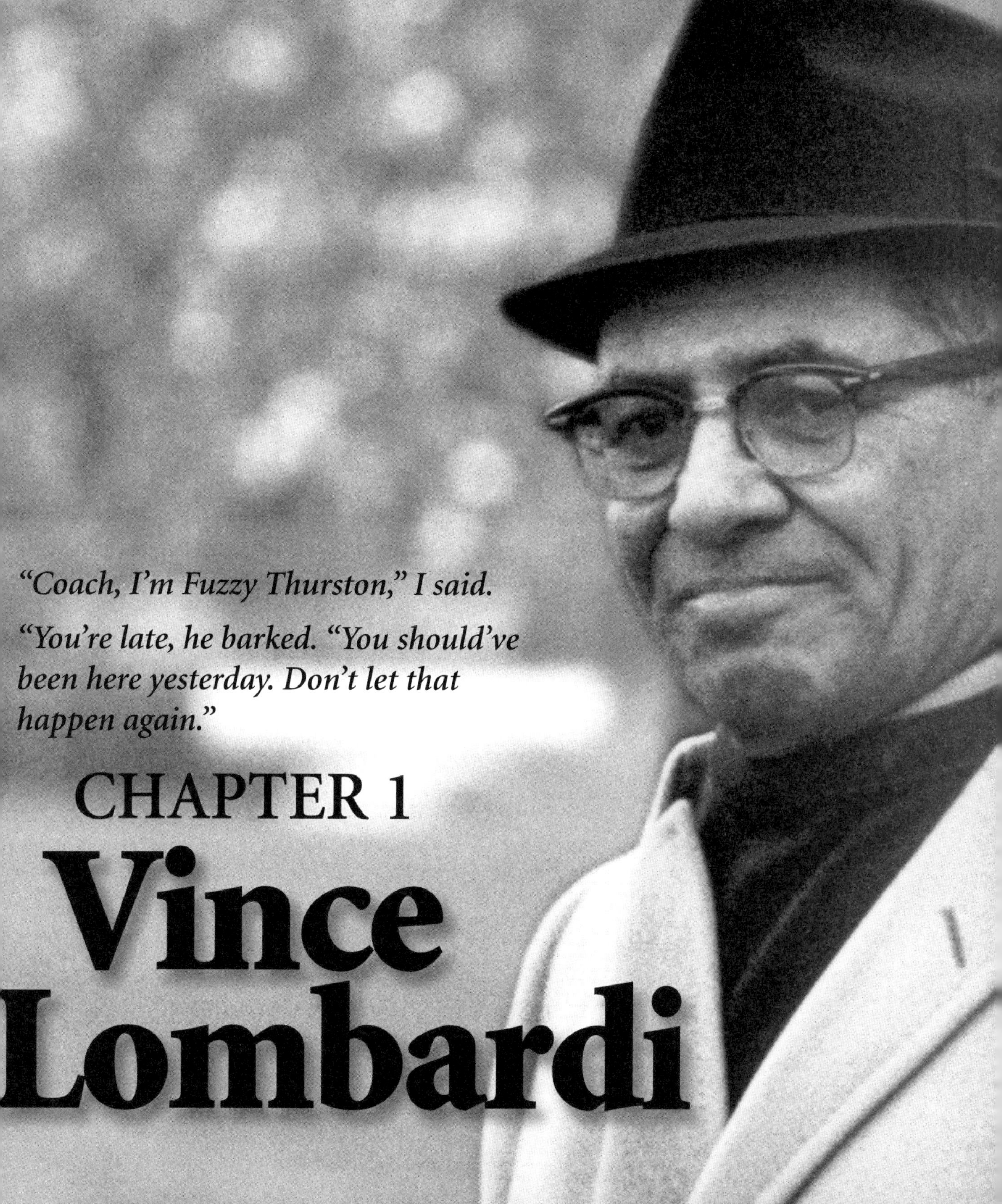

"Coach, I'm Fuzzy Thurston," I said.

"You're late, he barked. "You should've been here yesterday. Don't let that happen again."

CHAPTER 1
Vince Lombardi

He sized me up with those dark, penetrating eyes from across the empty locker room. He wasted no time issuing a question that sounded more like a challenge.

"Who the hell are you?" he shouted.

My new teammates had just left the locker room to hit the practice field for the morning workout, so I figured this was as good a time as any to introduce myself.

"Coach, I'm Fuzzy Thurston," I said.

"You're late," he said in an intimidating voice. "You should've been here yesterday. Don't let that happen again."

In the past 48 hours, I had witnessed the birth of my second son, driven from Madison to Baltimore and back again, and been traded by the Colts to the Packers in the process. I was tired. I was drained. I was running on fumes…but, I wasn't stupid. I stood up straight as an arrow, looked my new coach right in the eye and said, "Yes sir."

That was how I met Green Bay Packers Head Coach Vincent T. Lombardi, the man that would change my life forever. He wasn't interested in my circumstances, my situation, where I was born or why I wasn't on the practice field immediately after being traded to the Packers. No, Coach Lombardi wasn't interested in my life story. He was only interested in results.

When he told me never to be late again, I took it to heart and made a promise with myself to make sure it never happened. That's why, to this day, I'm 15 minutes early for everything. It is commonly referred to as "Lombardi Time." My wife can't stand it. Susan has been forced to be the first to baptisms, weddings, funerals and everything in between, almost always sitting out in the parking lot or the driveway with me waiting for the other guests to arrive. From the first day I met Coach Lombardi, I have been a fanatic with time, and continue to be to this day.

Vincent T. Lombardi was born on June 11, 1913 in Sheepshead Bay, New York, the son of a strict Catholic immigrant father. While growing up, Lombardi played football in prep school and later at Fordham University. He went on to coach high school football and eventually became an assistant coach at both Fordham University and the New York Giants. At the age of 46, he landed his first head coaching job in the NFL, with the Green Bay Packers. By the time he was done in Green Bay, Vince Lombardi coached the Green Bay Packers to 5 World Championships and 2 Super Bowl victories in nine seasons. Regarded by many as the greatest coach in NFL history, the "Vince Lombardi Trophy" is awarded to the Super Bowl champion each season.

Lombardi on the sideline with quarterback Ba

Coach Lombardi made an immediate first impression on the practice field. I was shocked. Here was this little man with intense eyes and a fiery temper, shouting at just about everyone in sight. And it was only practice. I knew right then that things were going to be really different. I had already played for great coaches, George Halas and Weeb Ewbank, but this guy was different. All I could think of at that moment was this guy meant business and I had better get my ass out on that field.

I read somewhere that Bob Long, a fine receiver and teammate of mine, said he spoke with Coach Lombardi perhaps 15 minutes during his four seasons in Green Bay. Fifteen minutes in four years. I bet Bob remembers each second to this day. His time was that precious. I know because I can still remember the rare occasions I got his attention.

So many players craved his attention. Maybe that's because we got so little of it, at least on a personal level. To Lombardi, you were just another football player. I do think that early on he knew I could really play football.

Vince Lombardi after Super Bowl I holds the trophy that would eventually bear his name.

Coach Lombardi was rough on us, but he was also extremely fair. It was like the great Henry Jordan said, "One good thing about Coach Lombardi is that he treats us all the same. He treats us like dogs." Every dog has his day, as they say, and one of mine came several years after I met Coach Lombardi.

We were in practice, working on our goal-line offense, and Coach Lombardi was a stickler about goal-line offense. He always said if we got within 5 yards of the end zone, we should never leave without scoring a touchdown. It's why we practiced it so much, and why he was pleased when we did it to perfection. Now, he didn't compliment anybody very often. And never, or almost never, did he compliment me. Well, we ran an off-tackle play, a trap, and I pulled and made a strong block that led to a touchdown.

Coach Lombardi jumped up, grabbed me and said, "Great, great block, Fuzzy!"

I said, "That's right, coach. They don't have to be tall to be great."

He laughed on that one, and he had a great laugh, which you didn't hear too often. So, whenever you got a laugh out of Coach Lombardi, everyone on the team noticed. I remember walking off the field after practice and Jerry Kramer coming over to me and draping a big arm around my shoulder. He said, "Hey, Fuzz, you got a laugh out of the old man. You're the king for the day." I was beaming inside and out. Those compliments were so few and far between that, when Coach Lombardi complimented you, you remembered them. I received a few compliments over the years, but none as good as that one.

Ron Kramer, our marvelous tight end, asked me one day, "Why do you show up? Coach is meaner to you, and tougher on you, than just about anybody else." Ron was right. Coach Lombardi probably was tougher on me than most. I didn't always understand it at the time, but looking back I think he had his reasons.

He was a guard. Lombardi left a prep school, where he was training to be a priest, for a school that would allow him to follow his passion for football. At Fordham University, he was one of the Seven Blocks of Granite, and he was little. I felt that, when I made that great block, it was important to him to see somebody like me, at my size, play well. He wanted me to do well. He made me a lot better football player than I would have been without him. As a player, he made me realize that I had to work hard, and that the harder I worked the better I would be. He also made me realize that it was not about me, it was about the team. Coach Lombardi preached that you were only as good as the guy next to you.

Coach Lombardi had a special theory about linemen. He felt they were the blood and guts of the offense. He wanted them to be tough and good, and he wanted to get more out of them than anyone else. The guards

Dan Grimm, Fuzzy Thurston and Bob Skoronski lead the way for running back Paul Hornung.

pulled on every play. Our whole scheme was the pulling guards in the offensive line. If we were going to be successful, the offensive line had to be up to the task. It was that simple.

He was tough on me, but he was tough on the whole offensive line. He realized how important it was to the football team. He realized if he was going to win in the National Football League, he had to have a running game. He didn't have many plays, maybe 40 or 50 pages, so he wasn't trying to outguess other teams. He wanted to outplay them. He wanted to out-execute them. He wanted to out-perfect and out-perform them.

Besides the passing game, we were going to run off tackle, or sweep, or maybe try a quick trap over the center, or a quick toss to one of backs. That was about it. The passing game was secondary.

The sweep was the signature play of the Green Bay Packers. In fact, the "Packers Sweep" was known and feared throughout the entire NFL. I was an important part of that play. Lombardi loved the sweep and in his system it was known as 49 "Red Right 49 on 2."

The sweep put the offensive guards on the map. Nobody knew Jerry Kramer and Fuzzy Thurston before the sweep became famous. We were the symbols, the pulling guards of the famous Lombardi sweep, and everyone knew our names.

I remember Lombardi first teaching us the sweep in a classroom setting, like a teacher, explaining it and dissecting it until we all understood it. He would make us run the play over 50 times a day in practice. It was the constant repetition that helped us execute the sweep to perfection on game day.

It was "repeat, repeat, repeat!" every day. Coach Lombardi never left anything to chance. He was so prepared. He was a great, great believer in this: If you don't make any mistakes, you won't lose any games. The plays were very basic, and execution was the key. Repetition was a big thing with him.

The structure under Coach Lombardi was straightforward. If it happened on offense, he knew about it. The defense he left to his coordinator, Phil Bengston, who ran it exclusively. The game management aspect was all

Lombardi and Starr watch the Packers' defense from the sidelines.

Lombardi, but he called very few plays. He left that to Bart Starr, and I don't think there ever was, or ever will be, a quarterback that called and played the game exactly as his coach wanted.

Everything Coach Lombardi told Bart in practice and meetings, Bart remembered in the game. Bart knew what coach wanted. He couldn't stress the running game any more than he did. If the sweep works, everything else works, because the defense had to spread the field. If we could run outside, we could run inside.

Bart's lack of an ego was also a key. He was a great quarterback for many reasons, but one of the most important was his basic understanding of what mattered. What's more important? Throwing the football or winning World Championships and Super Bowls? You had to sacrifice individual honors, and Bart did it like no one else.

While Bart was the triggerman, and perhaps more like Vince than the rest of us, Coach Lombardi knew it took all kinds of men coming together to build a winner. He understood, I think, before most of us, that there is strength in diversity. The problem is we were a little more diverse at times than Vince would have preferred.

One of those times came in December of 1962. We trampled the Los Angeles Rams, 41-10, in a game at Milwaukee's County Stadium to capture our third straight Western Conference championship. The next week we traveled to the West Coast for our annual road double-header at San Francisco (we beat the 49ers 31-21) and at Los Angeles (we got past the Rams 20-17).

It was our practice to stay on the West Coast for the entire two weeks. After defeating the 49ers we were feeling pretty good about our team, our 12-1 record and our chance to successfully defend our 1961 NFL Championship.

Naturally, we decided to celebrate, some of us more than others. We went out on the town with our wives and we did it up right. We went all out, and it was worth every minute, except for one small problem. We had practice the following day.

Coach Lombardi happened to be standing by the door when I boarded the team bus. He could smell the alcohol on me, the beer, as I was getting on. He didn't say a word, though, and we drove to a nearby college and had practice.

After practice, Coach Lombardi addressed the team briefly, and then he shouted, "Fuzzy, get on the goal line." He said, "Thurston, you're going to run some sprints." He didn't say what for, but everyone on the team knew it was because he caught a whiff.

I grabbed my helmet, took a deep breath and trotted toward the goal line. That's when a terrific thing happened. Coming right behind me were Paul Hornung, Max McGee, Boyd Dowler, my roommate Jesse Whittenton, Willie Wood, Herb Adderley, Jerry Kramer and Ron Kramer. Just about the whole damn team.

Coach Lombardi was already making his way to the locker room when he stopped, turned around and just shook his head. Then he growled, "Aw, the hell with it. Get your asses in the locker room and hit the showers!"

We just looked at each other and did as we were told. It made me feel so proud and so happy that my teammates thought so much of me. They were right there with me the night before, elbow to elbow at the bar, and they weren't going to let me take the heat all by myself. If we screw up, we screw up as a team. If we win, we win as a team. That's what was so great about that team. Besides, I didn't feel much like running, anyway.

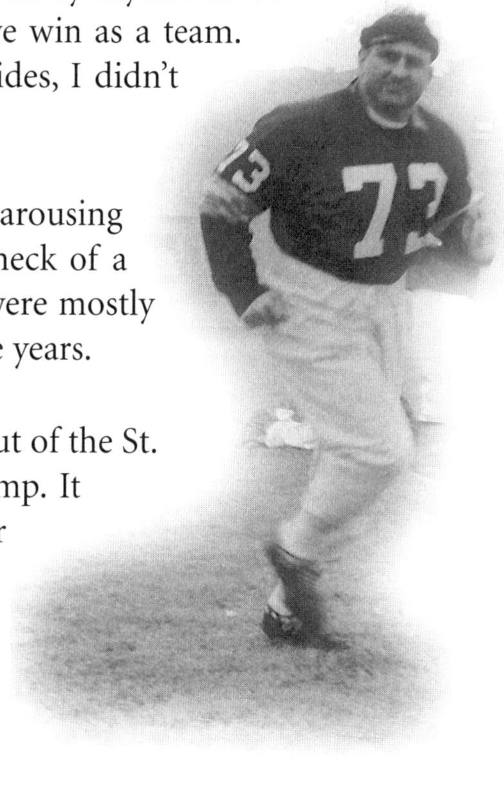

A lot has been written about our partying and carousing through the years, and we had ourselves one heck of a time, no doubt about it. But, those moments were mostly colorful stories that grew like a fish tale over the years.

However, I do recall the last time I ever snuck out of the St. Norbert College dormitory during training camp. It was '63 or '64 and we had been training hard for what seemed like all summer. Jesse Whittenton and I decided we deserved a break, which also meant we decided to sneak out after curfew.

About half an hour after bed check, we took off and hurried to a nearby bar. Lo and behold, of all the people in there, one of them is John "Red" Cochran, one of Coach Lombardi's assistants. Red and I were pretty close, so when he told us to get the heck back to the dormitory or else, we figured he was just bluffing. He'd never turn us in. So like two idiots we stayed.

We also paid the price the next morning. There was a knock on the door, and it was Coach Lombardi just glaring at us. He shook his head and said, "You guys are disgusting. I'll see you on the practice field." We had to run sprints until we were almost dead. It was 40-yard dashes, one after another, until we felt like we were going to be sick. We didn't get any help from our teammates that time.

It was the last time I ever left that dormitory. I didn't get enough sleep, I felt like you-know-what, and then I've got my boss upset and knocking down my door. I learned a valuable lesson, though: When a coach tells you to leave, you leave.

Do I think Coach Lombardi would

excel in today's NFL? I get that question a lot. I don't think he could have been like he was – I don't think the players would put up with it – but he would have been as close as he could have been to what he was. He would have gone as far as he could have gone, really pushed his players to the limit, and perhaps just a bit beyond. He also would have kept it simple. It still would have been running the football first and throwing it second, and I think he still would have been a winner. That wouldn't change.

Coach Lombardi demanded excellence and never accepted defeat. He was like a god to me, or maybe a dad, and even though he was tough on me, I always thought it was because he knew I could take it. My father died when I was four, and Vince was a huge influence on me. I really learned from his attitude and toughness.

Coach Lombardi had to have guys that he could use as an example to the other players. I just happened to be one of the examples he decided to use most. It was okay, though, because he had his reasons and we were winning. We had football by the throat. We were so talented. We were big across the entire nation. You couldn't have been bigger than the Packers after Super Bowl I.

That success inevitably led to some wonderful celebrations, and one of Coach Lombardi's favorite ways to celebrate was to have me sing. I learned another valuable lesson through the years: When Coach Lombardi tells you to sing, you sing. He would have me sing "He's got the whole world in his hands," although I would create my own verses.

Those were such great times, and everyone was so relaxed that we'd gather around and I would dedicate the song to a player, or the team, or the head coach. I would close it up with Vince, the man that made

Fuzzy Thurston, Paul Hornung and Max McGee sing a tune for the Coach.

this team the greatest, and I would sing, "He's got the whole football world in his hands. He's got the whole football world in his hands." And then I would throw in, "He's got the greatest guards in the world, in his hands. He's got the greatest guards in the world, in his hands." Unfortunately, my body gave out before my voice did.

After the 1968 season, I knew I didn't have much time left in the NFL. A year, perhaps, if that, but I wanted to play even though I wouldn't have been a starter. Gale Gillingham had taken my job. While I knew the end of my career was near, I also knew that I had accomplished so much. I was okay with retirement, thinking I had a bright future in the bar business. Retirement really scared my wife Sue, though, much more than me. I knew that Sue was really going to miss the game and the life of a player's wife.

I would have been the third guard, but that was all right. I was in the restaurant business throughout Wisconsin, and I figured another year would be good for business. Besides, I wasn't quite ready to hang it up.

This rare candid snapshot was taken at the 1968 1000-Yard Club Banquet where Vince told Fuzzy it was time to retire.

As it turned out, Coach Lombardi made the retirement decision for me. We were at the 1,000-yard Club Banquet and, in front of everyone, he asked, "Fuzzy, when are you going to announce your retirement?" I was shocked to hear those words come out of his mouth. As I said, I knew I would be retiring soon, but why did Coach Lombardi choose to inform me of his intentions in such a public place? It hurt, and it wasn't very respectful, but Coach Lombardi didn't have to be respectful to me. He said what he thought, and that was that. It wasn't long after that I did indeed decide to "officially" retire.

I think he liked me, though. Why wouldn't he like me? I was short, fast, hard working and got the job done.

Coach Lombardi stayed one year to be the Packers' general manager, but I never thought he would stay in that role for long. A year later, he left Green Bay to become the head coach and general manager of the Washington Redskins.

Vince Lombardi didn't return to Wisconsin, at least to speak publicly, until May of 1970. He was coming off a season in Washington that was much like his first season in Green Bay. There was no doubt Lombardi would whip the Redskins into Super Bowl champions. It was only a matter of time. The problem was, time was the one thing he didn't have.

My wife, Susan and I began hearing things about Coach Lombardi having health problems. The talk began circulating in mid-summer and it increased as the NFL season approached. By late July, it was obvious to those closest to him that he had colon cancer and was fighting for his life. The prognosis was grim, and I still remember hearing people say that this was an especially vicious form of cancer. I thought to myself that if anybody could beat the disease, it was Coach Lombardi.

It was in late August, I believe, when I got a telephone call from Bob Skoronski. My old line-mate said he had received a call from Marie Lombardi, and she said Vince wasn't doing very well. She also said that if we wanted to see him, we needed to get to Washington, D.C., sooner than later.

I was devastated. I didn't want to even think what it might be like without him. I just couldn't help thinking that, like my mother, he was leaving this world too soon. This couldn't be happening. He was so young, so powerful and so strong-willed. The word was that he was bad right from the start, and that he wasn't going to make it.

He was only 57.

Bob and I flew to D.C. and took a cab to Georgetown University Hospital, where Coach Lombardi had been admitted a second and final time. I cried even before I saw him. I knew he was experiencing some disorientation, and that he was terribly weak, but my greatest hope was that he would know who I am, and not yell at me.

When we got to the hospital, Marie met us and said, "Try not to be shocked." It was late in the afternoon, maybe 4 or 5 o'clock, when we went into his hospital room. Marie went into the room with us for a moment, but then she left. The room seemed incredibly small and crowded, even though it was just the three of us.

There were flowers in the room, and everything was so tidy, but Vince was remarkably frail. He weighed barely a hundred pounds. It was such a sad moment, but we were grateful to be able to say our good-byes. I just kept thinking over and over, this shouldn't be happening. He's just too young.

We told him that we loved him, that we respected him, and that we admired him as a coach, as well as a human being. We told him that all the yelling, screaming and good that he did for all his players was the reason we had such great success, why he was the great coach that he was, the greatest coach of all-time.

Coach Lombardi didn't say anything at first. Then he tried to say something, but couldn't, and summoned us closer.

Then, he said, "Boys, I don't think I can win this one."

And then the three of us cried. It was so sad, and so bad, and I kept thinking to myself, "How did he get so sick, so fast?"

Fans line up across the street from St. Patrick's Cathedral to pay their respects to the legendary coach. 3,000 mourners were in attend
INSET: Fuzzy Thurston and Max McGee attend Lombardi's fun

The flight to D.C. wasn't pleasant. The trip home was worse. We were anxious to see him, and we were so grateful for a chance to tell him how we felt, but when we said good-bye, we knew it was good-bye.

Coach Lombardi passed away a week later. That day, I reflected back on so many great moments we shared together. I still think of Coach Lombardi often.

I attended his funeral at St. Patrick's Cathedral in New York. More than three thousand mourners came to pay their final respects, the largest gathering at St. Patrick's since Robert Kennedy's funeral in 1968. It was so big and so busy, that it made me once again appreciate the chance to see him at the hospital one last time. It gave me one last chance to spend some very private time with the man who changed my life forever.

I had made peace with Coach Lombardi. After the funeral, in my mind and in my heart, I said, “Thanks, Coach. You’ll be okay where you’re going.”

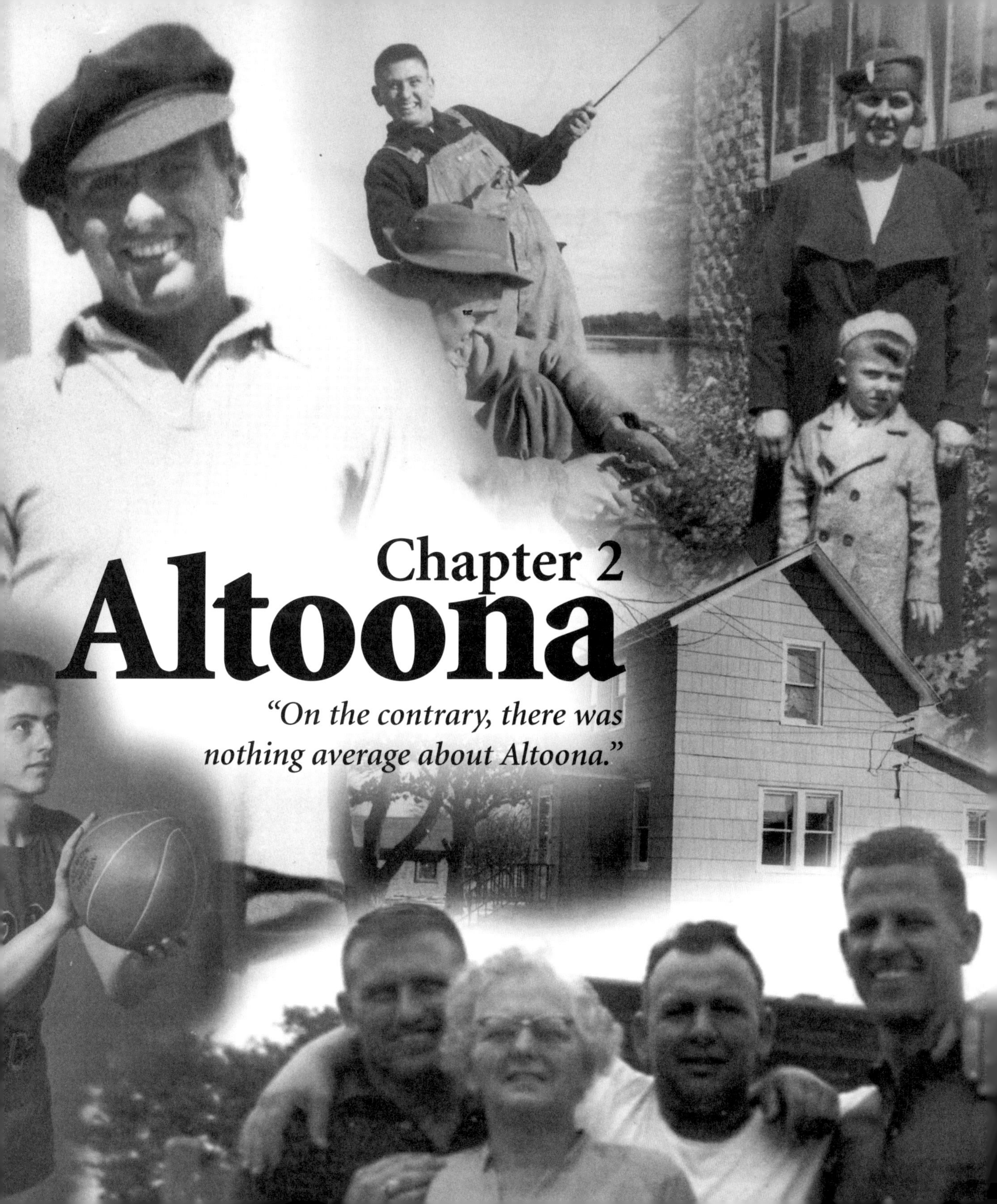

Chapter 2
Altoona

"On the contrary, there was nothing average about Altoona."

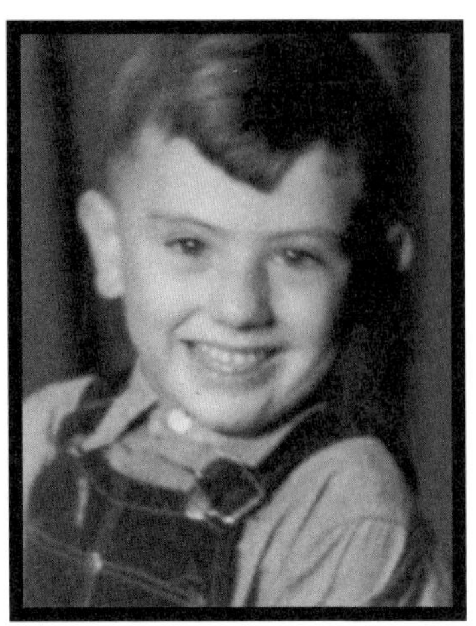

I was a happy boy. I had a loving mother and great brothers and sisters. From my perspective, at an early age, I had everything I needed in life. Looking back, I realize that I really didn't have much.

My father died when I was just four years old. Charles Warren Thurston was a 29-year-old laborer at Eau Claire Sand & Gravel when I was born, according to my birth certificate. It also states that I was 10 pounds, 22 inches, and that Marie Ernestina (Miller) Thurston, a 39-year-old housewife, brought me into this world at 3:20 p.m. on Dec. 29, 1933 at Luther Hospital in Altoona, Wisconsin.

What my birth certificate doesn't reveal is that Frederick Charles Thurston, the youngest of eight children, was the only one born in a hospital, and that my father died of a heart attack at 33. I have no recollection of my father. I had my brothers and sisters to take care of me. My brothers filled the void left by my father's death. Both had to quit school at a young age to help support the family.

Thurston's father died at the young age of 33, leaving the family very poor. This rare image is the only existing photograph of Charles Warren Thurston with Fuzzy.

Our family was very poor. We didn't have an indoor toilet until my junior year in high school. I don't remember getting much for Christmas because we didn't have any money for gifts. I don't remember doing much for Christmas, either, except walking the mile and a half to and from church and eating turkey instead of my mom's spaghetti. Spaghetti was a staple in our house because it was inexpensive to make.

Actually, it wasn't spaghetti, as you and I know it today. The recipe consisted of spaghetti noodles, tomato soup and cut up sausage links. Sometimes we would eat spaghetti four times a week. When we could afford it, we would have chicken on Sunday. We also ate a lot of noodles, potatoes, vegetables or whatever we could afford while I was growing up. I don't remember having meat very often at the dinner table, and when we did, there wasn't much to go around.

Altoona had three grocery stores back then. When anyone asks which store we shopped at, I tell them the same thing my best friend, Bob Thompson, would tell them: Whichever grocery store would give you credit.

I know we ate a lot of grapefruit. They called it "relief" at that time, and a guy would come around with fruit, flour and sugar. During the Great

Depression – and there was nothing great about it – my brother, Chuck, would gather coal from the coal cars or the coal piles in the nearby rail yard to heat our house during the winter.

For me, being poor and not having a father never really affected me. I didn't know any different. I had a basketball and a place to go shoot it. That was all I needed.

The Thurston family home in Altoona.

I grew up in a modest two-story home at 927 Hayden Avenue. It was two blocks from the nearest blacktop street, and a football field's length from the railroad tracks. The passenger trains were loud, and the freight trains were louder, but it wasn't so bad. When you live that close to the tracks, you quickly learn to tune out the noise. Besides, we didn't have too far to lug coal to keep from freezing in the winter.

My mother was a big, strong woman. She was very strict, but also very loving. She did what she had to do to keep our family going. She didn't remarry until ten years after my father died. She married a man named Peck Doughty, who was good to me for eleven months of the year. I didn't see him the other month because he was off on a binge. He was an alcoholic, but he only drank once a year for an entire month. Then he would sober up, go back to work and do the best he could for the next eleven months.

I had no real relationship with him. He didn't attend any of my basketball games or school functions. When he was drinking, he could be nasty. On many occasions, I remember him shouting profanities in the middle of the night, as we tried to sleep. Fortunately, he was a great provider for my mother. He was a hard worker and brought home a paycheck. The fact that he took care of my mother made up for the lack of a healthy relationship with him.

It wasn't ideal, but it wasn't the worst. It was what it was. I dealt with it, and I was always a happy-go-lucky kid.

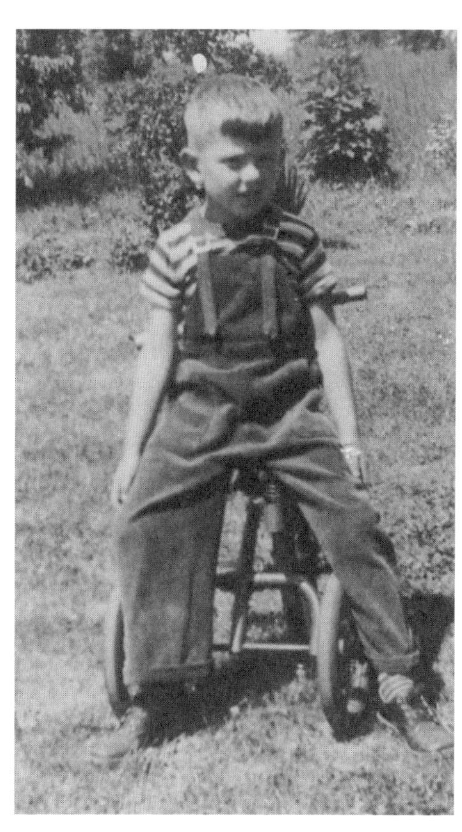

Mom was very strong-minded, and she loved her family first and foremost. I would call her strict with me because I was her baby. She wanted me to get an education, and she wanted me to succeed. She dedicated most of her life to make sure that I got what I needed.

She had dark hair, she was heavy for her height, and she had diabetes. She was supposed to watch what she ate, but she never did. Eventually, I was able to help her retire to Florida in her later years. She died a few days before Thanksgiving in 1962. She was 68. It was the worst day of my life. I owe everything I accomplished to her.

My mother was instrumental in making me aware of how difficult life could be. She told me to be happy as long as I had food on the table and a family to love. Life was very simple, but it wasn't easy. In fact, it was very difficult. It was still enjoyable, though, and my mother made it that way. I'm so grateful for what my mother taught me. I learned how to be happy

Fuzzy and his mother share a special moment.

and stay strong in whatever circumstances I was faced with.

That isn't to say she didn't have to make some difficult choices along the way. When I was twelve, my mother couldn't afford to take care of me. Unselfishly, she put me on a train to Lutz, Florida. I lived with my aunt Lillian, worked in the orange groves and attended sixth grade. I grew up a lot that year. From that experience, I learned I could take care of myself, and I enjoyed the responsibility.

I knew I would be coming back home in a year. I missed my friends, but I knew it would help my family financially. For my mother, it was one less mouth to feed. It was not as upsetting as you might think. In some ways, it was exciting for me. I was going to Florida, and that was an adventure. I was away from my friends for that whole year, but I was the kind of kid that adjusted really well to whatever situation came along.

When I returned to Altoona, I began constantly shooting baskets on the hoop at Darrell Woodington's gas station. The Woodingtons were a great family, and Darrell was a nice man. He enjoyed making Altoona a little bit nicer for the kids, even if it was doing something as seemingly small as putting up a basketball hoop. It may not have been a big deal to anyone else in town, but to us kids it was the greatest.

I kept on shooting at Woodington's hoop because I had decided by the seventh grade that athletics might be my only ticket out of town. I respected what the railroad meant to my hometown's past, present and future, but I had no intention of living in Altoona and working on it. I wanted something different for myself, and what's more, my family wanted something better for me. I was the baby of the family, and my brothers and sisters were determined to help me succeed.

None of my brothers and sisters graduated from high school. They quit school and went to work because our mother needed their help, and because they wanted to give me a chance to earn a high school diploma, go to college, and have a better life. They loved me, and I loved them.

They sacrificed a lot for me. The fact that they didn't graduate from high school didn't embarrass me. It motivated me. I didn't want to let them down, so I shot baskets at Woodingtons, I studied, and I did my homework. I worked at trying to earn a basketball scholarship to the University of Wisconsin-Eau Claire. I dreamed of becoming a high school teacher and a basketball coach.

My heroes were the Wisconsin Badgers football and basketball players that received write-ups in the local newspaper, the Eau Claire-Leader Telegram. I was a big Wisconsin fan, and I still am. When I was a kid in Altoona, I thought how great it would be if just once I got to attend a Badgers football or basketball game in Madison.

The Railroaders, Fuzzy's high school basketball team. Fuzzy is bottom row, third from the

The Green Bay Packers weren't very good at the time, as I recall, and nobody in Altoona spent a great deal of time talking about them. I never imagined that one day I would play for the Packers. I would have been happy just to go to a Packers game.

While I worked and dreamed, my family cheered at my basketball games, cried at my graduation ceremony, and was proud knowing I was going to college. The UW-Eau Claire Blugolds had no interest in me as a basketball player, but Valparaiso did. When I graduated, I was off to Indiana to attend college.

I felt blessed because every member of my family sacrificed something to help me. I owed all of them. I could see it in their eyes that they accomplished what they set out to do. With their love and support, I felt like anything was possible. Their love and sacrifices have stayed with me all my life, giving me the confidence I needed to succeed and persevere through life.

Einar Pedersen, my first basketball coach, was also a big influence in my life. He was an excellent coach and a positive influence. He was a good role model for me, and I was impressed with his positive attitude and work ethic. I wanted to be like him, and he was one of the biggest reasons I wanted to play college basketball. I played guard as a high school freshman on Mr. Pedersen's team.

My two eldest sisters are still alive. Dorothy is 90 and Evelyn is 86. The five others (Ruth, Jane, Chuck, Jim and an older brother that died on the railroad) have passed away.

Dorothy, because she was the oldest, did a great deal to help raise me. She also is responsible for giving me my nickname. She would rub my head when I was a toddler and say, "Oh, his hair is so fuzzy." She said it so often that it wasn't long before everyone in the house was calling me Fuzzy. Everyone, that is, except my mother. She was the only person in the world that called me Fritzy, and I'm still not sure why. To everyone else, I was Fuzzy.

In a small town like Altoona, where everybody knows everybody, you have to figure a nickname like that is going to stick. Oh, Fuzzy stuck all right. I thought it was a goofy name. Certainly not a name for a tough, strong athlete like myself.

I was a rough-and-tumble kid and big for my age. I broke Ray Henning's arm sliding into second base at a softball game during recess. I felt bad for Ray, who was a friend, but not nearly as bad as I felt for myself a few years later when I ran into Ray's cousin, Ione, at Valparaiso University.

Ione was bright, outgoing, and happy to see anyone from her hometown. She was a cheerleader at Valparaiso. She had long since forgotten Ray's broken arm, but she remembered me. When she saw me she shouted, "Hi, Fuzzy! It's great to see you."

It was great seeing Ione, too, except for one problem. Several of my teammates heard her call me Fuzzy. To them, I was simply Fred Thurston. They had never heard anyone call me Fuzzy. They fell down laughing and teased me mercilessly, but it wasn't long before they started calling me Fuzzy the same as my buddies back home.

I had great friends growing up, but Bob Thompson was my best friend. He hurt his back in a serious bicycle accident when he was young, so he couldn't play sports for several years while recovering. Bob didn't complain, though. He became the team manager. He wrapped my ankles and applied Tuff-skin to the souls of my flat feet so they wouldn't be tender.

We're still best friends to this day. Bob and his wife, Shirley, and my wife Sue and I have spent a great deal of time together through the years. Sue and Shirley were friends before I met Sue. They lost touch briefly, but when they got reacquainted they also got a pleasant surprise. Shirley had married Bob, my best friend, and the four of us have been close friends ever since.

Bob came to a great many Packers games during my career, and he enjoyed the victories and the celebrations almost as much as I did. It was special for me to be able to share such wonderful moments with my best friend from grade school. The NFL and Altoona seemed worlds apart. Bob helped bridge the gap.

To this day, we still enjoy getting together for a few drinks and singing the great Altoona High School cheer. It goes like this:

"Engine, Boxcar, Baggage Car, Caboose. ... Come on team, we're cutting loose. Chug-chug, chug-chug, chug-chug, chug! Woo! Woo! Altoona!"

It never fails to bring down the house at my bar, Fuzzy's 63, or to prompt Bob and I into reminiscing about the good old days.

Altoona didn't have the boys or the budget to field a high school football team, so Bob and I played pickup football games in the sandlots. Bob was always Glen Davis, the Army fullback, and I was always Doc Blanchard, the Army halfback, and we never lost.

When we reached junior high, we played St. Benedict's Boys School in a sandlot football game once or twice a year. St. Benedict's was a home for troubled boys from throughout the Midwest. Nuns ran St. Benedict's, which was only a few blocks from my house, and I befriended several of the boys there. The gym at our high school was too small for seating, so we practiced there and played our games at the city auditorium.

Looking back on growing up in Altoona, I was the average all-American boy. By average, I mean just that. Average. I wasn't great at anything.

On the contrary, there was nothing average about Altoona. Its population was about 1,100 when I was growing up. Today it's 6,700. Back then it featured three bars, a post office and rooms for rent to the railroad workers. The 400 Club, The Golden Spike, and The Rail Haven were the three bars that catered to the townsfolk and railroad workers alike. Altoona has been described as a Peyton Place because of its transient work force, its good natured and occasionally down-and-dirty bars, and the potential for illicit trysts because of the two.

Dolly McKeeth, a tough-as-she-had-to-be proprietor, owned and operated Dolly's restaurant. She cooked the food, waited on the tables, cleaned up and closed up. Then, the next day, she opened up and started all over again. She worked there for an amazing number of years without missing a single day. She was rough like the toughest little lady you could imagine from an old Western movie, but she also had a heart of gold... and the best damn chicken you ever tasted!

Sue, my wife, grew up in Eau Claire, and like many of her friends, her parents strongly discouraged her from visiting Altoona because of its reputation as a rough town. That didn't stop Sue and her friends from frequenting The Golden Spike, and while I can't recall having any trouble, I can't honestly say the potential didn't exist.

One of the best things about Altoona, is that's where I met my wife Sue. It has been said that life is a beach, which is where I first met Sue. For much of the past fifty years, our life together has been like a day at the beach. For Sue and I, it was love at first sight. Our love for each other has grown deeper through the years, during good times and bad.

I met Sue in the summer of 1956. I had just graduated from Valparaiso University. I was a fourth round draft pick of the Philadelphia Eagles, which was very high because there were only twelve NFL teams at that time. I still lived in Altoona, working out and getting ready for the upcoming NFL season. I wanted to be in great shape for training camp with the Eagles. Sue lived in Eau Claire, just a few miles from Altoona.

I had a routine that summer. I would work out during the day and go out at night. One afternoon, I was running on the beach and nearly ran into Sue and one of her girlfriends. I said, "Hi, I'm Fuzzy. What's your name?" Most sports fans in the area knew who I was, so it bothered me that she didn't

Fuzzy with his future wife Sue.

know who I was. Sue told me later that she DID know who I was from reading about me in the Eau Claire Leader – Telegram. She just pretended she didn't recognize me because she could tell it bothered me. We didn't say much beyond the introduction. We both went out with our friends that night to an Altoona bar called the Golden Spike, but we didn't talk much there, either.

A few nights later, I ran into Sue at a bar called the Hoot. It was a beer bar for anyone eighteen years or older, but I didn't go there just to drink. I went to dance. There was great music on the jukebox. We would do the jitterbug, and if you got serious with a girl, you'd slow dance. Sue and I weren't at that point. Not yet, anyway.

After a while, I finally got up the nerve to ask Sue to dance. She told me later that she thought to herself, "Oh brother, this could be the longest dance in the world." Not to brag, but I am a really good dancer. I am a

big guy, but light on my feet. As it turned out, Sue and I could have danced all night. Sue gave me her telephone number at the end of the night.

I waited two days to call her. I was really excited to be going out on our first date when I went over to Sue's house to pick her up. Her Dad was a high school football coach, and he moonlighted as a high school basketball referee. He actually worked about fifteen of my games and fouled me out of every game! That's the God's honest truth. He loved the way I played the game because I was "aggressive as hell." Her mother, on the other hand, looked at my bib overalls and torn white T-shirt and must have thought, "What is Sue getting herself into?"

Sue and I went out that night, and we kept going out as often as possible. It was a serious relationship right from the beginning. It was really amazing. I was constantly telling Sue how much I loved her and how pretty she was. Through the years, I try to compliment Sue on a regular basis, which makes her feel good.

Right from the start, Sue and I had a terrific attraction for each other. However, it was more than just that. We had so much fun together. We talked, we laughed and we danced together often. We really enjoyed each other's company, and we were both very respectful of our parents and family. I liked everything about Sue.

Shortly after we started going out, I had to leave for the Philadelphia Eagles

Training Camp. I kept in touch by mail. Sue told me that the "beautiful letters" I sent made her love me even more. We didn't see each other much, but still we grew closer. I was cut by the Eagles and immediately drafted by the United States Army.

I remember Sue saying good-bye as I boarded the bus for boot camp. We were both sad that I was leaving again. We continued our long distance relationship while I was at boot camp, and our bond continued to strengthen. I really missed her. I knew that I wanted to spend the rest of my life with her. During one of my military leaves, I asked Sue to marry me.

We got married on October 3, 1956 in Eau Claire at the First Lutheran Church with many friends and relatives in attendance at both the wedding and reception. We had a short, two-day honeymoon in the Twin Cities, and then it was back to the Army. This time, Mrs. Susan Thurston was coming with me.

I remember that Sue wanted to impress my Army buddies. Trying to look her best, she decided to work on her tan on the way back to Texas. We had the top down on the convertible through the whole state of Arkansas. She arrived with a huge blister on her forehead. It was so bad I had to take her to the emergency room to have it lanced! So much for first impressions!

The Thurston Family, Tori, Fuzzy, Mark, Sue and Griff.

We lived in newlywed bliss on the base in San Antonio, Texas. In May of 1958, Mark, our first of three children, was born. Our son Griff, followed in July of 1959. Finally, our beautiful daughter Tori was born in November of 1962. Who would have imagined that the night of dancing at The Hoot in Altoona would turn into a loving fifty- year relationship with my wife and three beautiful children.

Altoona was and still is referred to as "the end of the line." Years ago, 100 miles constituted a day's work on the railroad, and Altoona was about 100 miles south of Spooner, 100 miles southeast of St. Paul, and 100 miles northwest of Adams-Friendship. After a 100-mile day, the railroad workers had a full day's work in, thus making Altoona "the end of the line."

The 400 Club was named after "The 400," a passenger train that could travel from Chicago to St. Paul in approximately 400 minutes.

The roundhouse in the rail yard was a hub of activity. It was there that the trains were repaired, restocked and redirected.

The icehouse was critical to the railroad's success. The ice was used to refrigerate whatever produce, meat or poultry was being shipped. The ice came in 250-pound blocks, and it required a strong back to heft it onto the chute leading into the refrigeration car.

I worked in the icehouse during the summers between my freshman and senior years at Valparaiso. I packed on pounds of muscle each summer, and nearly ate my mother out of house and home. Those summers helped prepare me for what was to come.

My final summer at Valparaiso, I worked as a laborer on a construction crew that was building new dormitories on campus and I added more muscle that summer.

I weighed 155 pounds when I graduated high school, but by the time the Philadelphia Eagles selected me in the fourth round of the 1955 draft, I was a strapping 240 pounds. I played at 260 pounds during my best years with the Packers, but I have no doubt that those grueling summers made all the difference in the world.

By the time I got to the NFL, I was ready to play with the big boys, and as much as I hated working at the icehouse in Altoona, I appreciated the good it did for me. The most important lesson learned at the icehouse

Fuzzy and his Valparaiso teammates. Fuzzy is third from the right.

was that I did not want to do this the rest of my life. The experience served as great motivation to get an education.

They didn't have a football team when I attended Altoona High School, but they do now, and the Railroaders play on a field that is named for me.

The sign reads: ***Fred "Fuzzy" Thurston Football Field***
Dedicated By The Class Of 1951
#63 Left Guard 1959-1967
GREEN BAY PACKERS

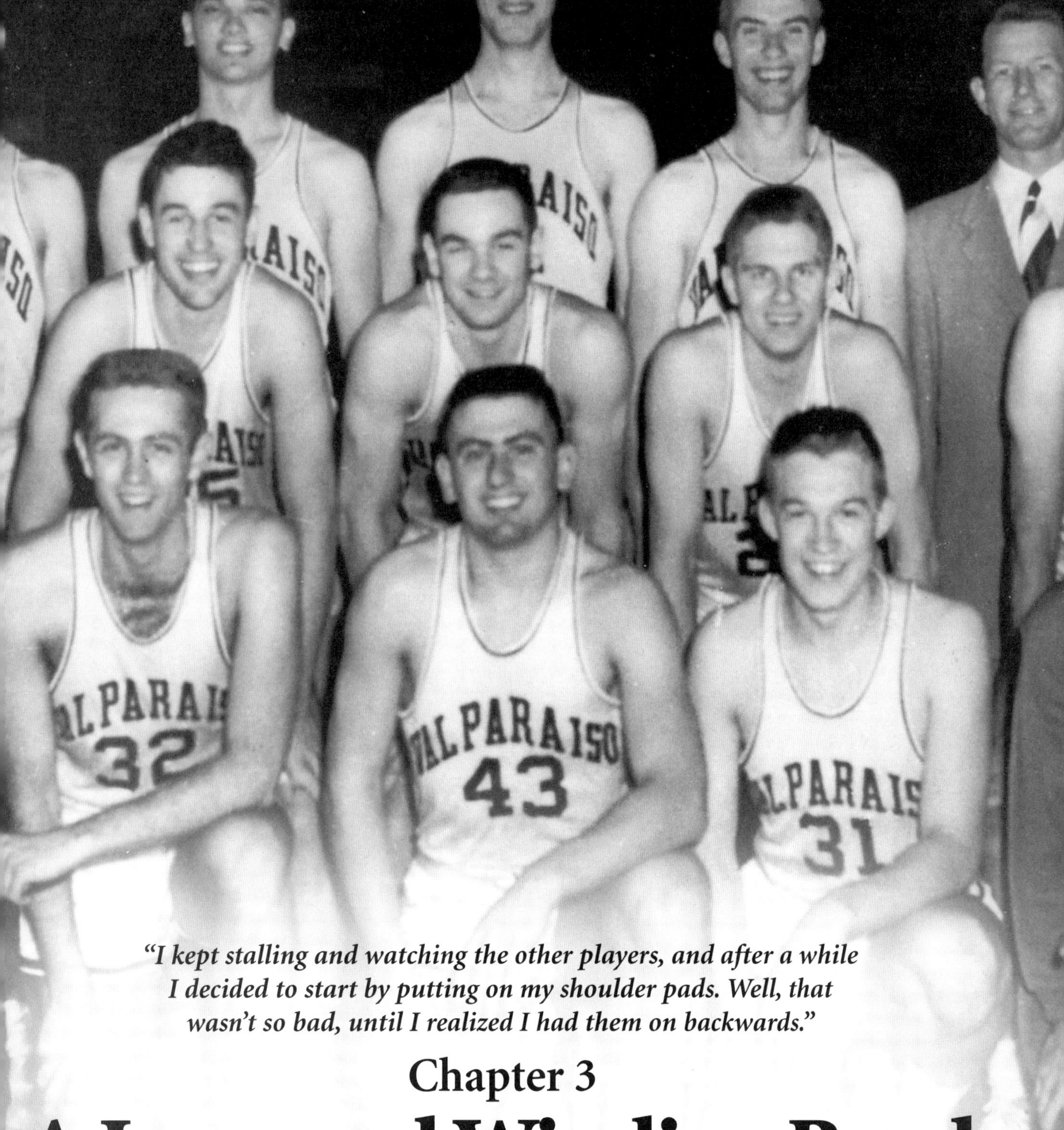

"I kept stalling and watching the other players, and after a while I decided to start by putting on my shoulder pads. Well, that wasn't so bad, until I realized I had them on backwards."

Chapter 3

A Long and Winding Road

It was the spring semester of my sophomore year at Valparaiso University. I was sitting in one of Walt Reiner's Physical Education classes, trying to concentrate on the material, but thinking about my next basketball game, when Reiner asked to see me after class.

I didn't think I was in trouble because my grades were OK, and I had always gotten along well with Reiner, who was the assistant football coach, so I wasn't sure what he wanted. The mystery was solved in a single sentence.

"Fred," Reiner said. "I've been watching you play basketball for almost two years now, and I have decided you could be one hell of a football player."

Valparaiso was a small school in Indiana. There was an unwritten rule that the football and basketball coaches wouldn't try to recruit players from each other's team. As Reiner later explained it to me, "We tried to be nice to each other. Well, two years of being nice was about all I could stomach. Finally, I told myself, 'That's enough.' We had this guy (Thurston) who weighed 230 pounds, could high jump six feet with no trouble, threw all the weights in track, and was exceptionally strong and agile. The football field seemed like the place for him."

I was 19 years old. I had never played organized football, except for some sandlot football while growing up in Altoona, but I always liked all sports. It's just that I spent 12 months out of the year practicing basketball, so it was the only sport I really knew how to play.

Football interested me, though. It was kind of fun to get involved after all these years of just watching. I was an aggressive basketball player, rough-and-tumble just like when I was a kid, and I was curious about the physical aspect of football.

Valparaiso was having spring football practices, and I was going to give it a try. Coach Reiner and I spent quite a bit of time together covering the basics, everything from rules and plays to the fundamentals of blocking and tackling.

I immediately fell in love with football. I was so excited the night before our first practice I could hardly sleep. I kept wondering how I would do against guys that had been playing for years. I wasn't worried, though. I was eager because I knew I could compete athletically, and part of me wondered if maybe I just might have found my best sport.

Everything went well the first day. That is, until my teammates started putting on the pads. As I looked around the locker room, I looked at my pads and realized I had no idea how to properly put them on. It was embarrassing. I kept stalling and watching the other players, and after a while I decided to start by putting on my shoulder pads. Well, that wasn't so bad, until I realized I had them on backwards.

Coach Reiner must have sensed my frustration because he came over and made a joke about how that stuff happens all the time. Then he helped me into my pads after most of my teammates were already on the practice field.

The shoulder pads felt uncomfortable – even after they were properly in place – and the helmet was even worse. It seemed so bulky and heavy and out of place that I didn't think I would ever get used to it.

Thank goodness I was a lot more comfortable on the practice field. I had never been in a three-point stance or tackled someone – unless it was while diving for a loose basketball or in a sandlot football game – but it came together very quickly. I loved the contact, and I loved the camaraderie, and that wouldn't change.

Coach Reiner put me on defense. He felt I could best utilize my strength, agility and athleticism at defensive end. I was 6-foot-1, weighed about 230 pounds, and was probably the best natural athlete on the team from day one.

I quickly learned that football, like basketball, was all about balance. You couldn't make a block or a tackle if you were on the ground. The fact that I had played basketball for so long, and that I was used to being in a defensive stance or making sharp cuts on offense, really paid off.

I played defensive end in the spring, but Coach Reiner moved me to the offensive line before the start of the season. They needed help on the line, and they put me at left tackle, where I could run block or protect the quarterback's blind side on pass plays. I had a whole two weeks to get ready for the opening game. Thanks to Coach Reiner, I was ready, and a football career was born.

I had a terrific football career at Valparaiso. I was named to the All-Conference Team after my first two seasons, and I was beginning to draw interest from NFL scouts. Coach Reiner told me that I might have a chance to play in the NFL, but it would be wise to play a third season in college. So, instead of graduating in the spring of '55, I got a summer job in Valparaiso working on a construction crew that was building dormitories.

During the day, I pushed wheelbarrow after wheelbarrow of concrete up a ramp. I was a laborer and it was hot, hard work, but it made me that much tougher and stronger. In the evenings, after it cooled down, Coach Reiner and I would go to the track. He would have me stretch, run 40-yard dashes, and then the mile. Afterward, we would talk at length about football. I couldn't have been better prepared as a fifth-year senior.

star in the making. Fuzzy is the feature player on the cover of a 955 Valparaiso game program.

I had a strong season and I was beginning to be noticed. I was voted the Most Valuable Player of our conference, an award that had always gone to a quarterback, running back or receiver – one of the skill positions – but never an offensive lineman. There was talk that I might be drafted by an NFL team, which was unheard of for a player from

Valparaiso. Coach Reiner continued to encourage me. He kept telling me, "We've got something special here."

Coach Reiner was right. The Philadelphia Eagles selected me in the fourth round of the 1956 NFL draft. There were 12 teams in the league at that time, which meant I was one of the Top 50 players selected overall. That's quite an honor for a left tackle from Valparaiso.

Someone from the Eagles' front office, an assistant GM, called and told me that they had drafted me. He said they would send an offer in the mail. When I got the offer, I called the Eagles and tried to negotiate a little bit. In those days, players did not have agents. In fact, I never had an agent throughout my entire NFL career. I asked for a $500 bonus to sign. I didn't know any pro football players, and my college coach had no idea what I should ask for, but it didn't really matter. The Eagles, in plain English, told me that they "didn't give bonuses unless you were picked in the first round. However, if you don't make the team, we will pay for you to fly back home to Wisconsin."

I agreed and that was the end of the negotiation. I signed my first NFL contract for $5,000. I was thrilled to be drafted, and I just knew I would make the team. What I didn't know is that it would be nearly three years before I played in an NFL regular season game. I would be drafted twice in 1956, first by the Eagles, and then by the United States Army.

I reported to the Eagles' training camp in '56, lined up at left guard, and played in three exhibition games. I got kicked out of the first exhibition game, my first game in the NFL, for fighting. A defensive end slugged me, and I thought 'If that's how it is, then that's how it is.' So, I slugged him back. The official didn't see the first punch (they never do), but he saw the second one and I got ejected.

Afterward, I felt awful. I thought the Eagles might cut me right then and there. I felt a little better when some of the veterans came up, patted me on the back and said, "You did the right thing, Fuzzy. Don't take any shit from anyone." The veterans liked me for it.

Training camp and the exhibition games were going well, and the highlight was getting to play against the Pittsburgh Steelers' Ernie Stautner. Stautner, now a member of the Pro Football Hall of Fame, was a 6-foot-2, 235-pound tackle. He was tough as nails. He also had an eye for the ladies.

In the team hotel the day before the game, Stautner and some of his Steelers teammates were hanging out in the lobby. I was impressed with the players' size, and the fact that Stautner was flirting with my girlfriend, Sue.

The game was in Minneapolis, so Sue and her parents made the trip from Eau Claire to watch me play. When Stautner was flirting with Sue I didn't get jealous. Actually, I felt pretty good. I figured if Ernie Stautner thought she was really something, I must've been doing something right.

Stautner was great for my confidence on the field, too. I knew how good he was and that he was an All-Pro. In fact, he was named the NFL's Best Lineman in 1957, the year after we met in the exhibition game. Well, I blocked Stautner that game, and after that I knew I could play in the NFL.

It meant a lot because every time I was released or traded I never got down. I was always optimistic because I knew I was good enough. I had gone one-on-one with Ernie Stautner, and I had more than held my own. No matter what happened, I knew I wasn't going to quit.

It wasn't easy, though. After the Steelers exhibition game, I rode with Sue and her parents to Eau Claire, and I went to see my mother in Altoona. She had something for me when I arrived. It was a draft notice from the Army. I had one more exhibition game with the Eagles, and about a week to report to Fort Chaffee, Arkansas, for basic training.

I never played that final exhibition game because the Eagles cut me. I was so hurt and so down, and I was staring at two years of military duty. Somehow, I kept my spirits up because I still believed I would make it in the NFL. It was never a matter of whether I could play. It was only a question of when.

I promised myself to make the best of my time in the Army. The pay in the military wasn't very good, just barely enough to live on. Of course, I was no stranger to that situation. To supplement my meager income, I worked part-time cleaning the movie theatre and bathrooms. It wasn't fun, but I was able to take Sue to the movies for free and make a few extra dollars.

In the end, my experience in the military proved invaluable. In addition to my assigned duties, I wrestled and played football for the Army. I played left tackle. During the next 21 months I honed my skills, polished my technique and absorbed a great deal of football knowledge.

The quality of football was better than I had seen at Valparaiso, probably on par with the Big Ten, but not nearly as good as the NFL. By the time my hitch was up, I had made a name for myself and was fairly respected by several NFL players in the service.

The Bears' Harlon Hill, who I met while in the service in San Antonio, put me in touch with owner George "Papa Bear" Halas, who later signed me in May of 1958. I finally got the $500 bonus I wanted two years earlier. That was a lot of money in those days, but more importantly, I had a job in the NFL.

The Bears put me at defensive end, and, while I felt the offensive line was my best position, I went where I was told. They had a future Pro Football Hall of Fame defensive end, Doug Atkins, and several other very good players at the position.

I played stand-up defensive end for three exhibition games with the Bears, then I was traded back to the Philadelphia Eagles for a conditional, undisclosed draft pick. I was okay with it because I figured, "If Philadelphia traded for me, and I was going there for a second time, it must mean that they really want me."

The Eagles penciled me in at left guard. I started and ran with the first team, and I thought, "Finally, I have a home." I was wrong, again.

On the Wednesday before the regular-season opener, the Eagles informed me that they were going to release me. Maybe it was because they didn't think I could play. Maybe it was because they didn't want to send a draft pick to the Bears. I'll never know because nobody was saying and the terms of the deal were never made public.

I still had confidence, though. I felt like it wasn't my problem. They were the ones that had made the mistake, and I haven't liked Philadelphia to this day. I would have been the water boy if it meant being in the NFL. Now, I was unemployed, married to Sue and the proud father of a four month old son. I didn't have time to feel sorry for myself.

Soon thereafter, the Winnipeg Blue Bombers of the Canadian Football League called and asked if I would sign there. I needed a job and the money, so I packed up Sue, my son Mark, and drove to Winnipeg.

On our way out of Philadelphia I turned the radio on. It was the Eagles' season opener, a game that I should have been playing in, and I was upset. Needless to say, Sue and I were cheering for whoever the Eagles were playing that day.

My time in Canada was short, but valuable. I was there a week, but before I signed a contract, the Bombers' Head Coach, Bud Grant, called me into his office. Grant said the Baltimore Colts called and inquired about signing me to a contract. He said he hated to do it, because he really wanted me, but he felt I needed to go to Baltimore and give it another try. He told me he felt I belonged in the NFL, and that if I was given another chance I could have a good career.

Grant was quiet, strong and very impressive. I can never thank him enough for his candor and honesty.

Once again, I was on the road. I drove to Green Lake, Wisconsin to drop Sue and Mark at her parent's house. Then, I flew to Baltimore. I was excited and I was nervous, but most of all, I was bound and determined to make my mark in the NFL.

Colts Head Coach Weeb Ewbank signed me to the taxi squad, which is similar to today's practice squad. I practiced with the team, made friends and waited for my chance to play. It came after six weeks when the Colts activated me for the Green Bay game. As a Wisconsin native, I was excited to be playing against the Green Bay Packers. I still loved the Packers, even when I was playing against them. I couldn't help but think to myself, 'thank God

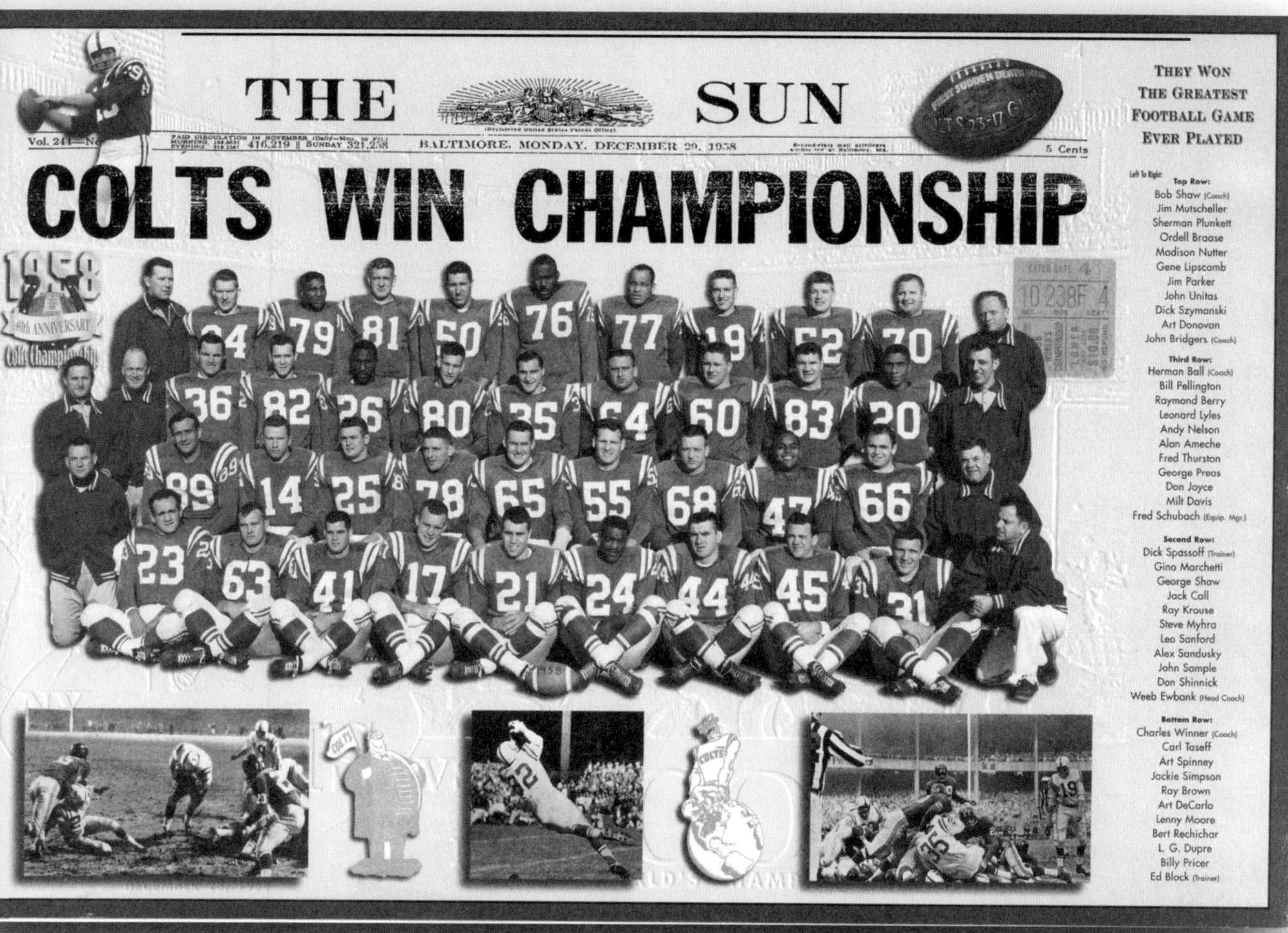

Third row, fifth from right: #64 Fuzzy Thurston when he was a member of the World-Champion Baltimore Colts team.

I play for the Colts.' The Packers were not very good at that time.

The Colts beat the Packers, 56-0, and I didn't know whether I felt sorrier for the Packers or the Colts' mascot, a horse, that ran around the field every time we scored. I thought that poor horse was going to die from exhaustion. I was playing special teams, but the Colts were winning so big I played left guard the last two series of the game.

I was enjoying being in Baltimore, and we were winning. The Colts finished 9-3 to win the Western Conference title, and then they went on to beat the New York Giants 23-17 in the World Championship. I couldn't have been happier.

I enjoyed playing special teams and I was good at it. I liked to tackle, probably from my days at Valparaiso as a defensive end, and I knew the coaches were impressed with my attitude and my hustle.

My prospects of becoming a starter with the Colts were good. Both of the starting guards, Steve Myhra and Alex Sandusky, were older players. I knew it was only a matter of time, maybe a year or two, before I would work my way into the starting lineup.

The Colts were awfully talented, too. They had greats such as Johnny Unitas, Raymond Berry, Lenny Moore, Gino Marchetti, Art Donovan, Big Daddy Lipscomb and Jim Parker.

After all of my travels and problems, I finally made it. I was on a championship team, and we had great offensive talent in its prime. I felt like I was a millionaire.

Sue and Mark were living in Green Lake, but we moved to Madison when I enrolled in order to pursue my Master's degree in Physical Education. I wanted to have it, just in case something happened with football, so I could still become a teacher and coach if necessary.

Life was good. I enjoyed being in Madison. Mark was healthy and Sue was pregnant with our second child. Naturally, I was thrilled to be playing with the Colts for a couple of reasons.

First, since we won the World Championship the previous season, we would be playing against the college stars in the NFL-College All-Star Game in

Chicago. That was especially exciting to me, coming from a small school like Valparaiso University, and I couldn't wait to test myself against the best and brightest.

Second, I was penciled in to start at one of the guard spots, probably on the left side, for Coach Weeb Ewbank's Colts. I was eager to be blocking for future Pro Football Hall of Fame players, such as quarterback Johnny Unitas and halfback Lenny Moore, and along the same offensive line as big Jim Parker, our left tackle. It wasn't meant to be, which isn't surprising, really, because my whole football career is so unusual the way it happened.

It was July 17, 1959, the day before I was to drive to Baltimore for training camp, when Sue gave birth to a beautiful son, Griff, and I was in my glory. Susan and I were so thrilled with the birth of our second son, and we were eager to make Baltimore our home. After he was born, I drove all night to Baltimore and I was just happier than hell. I got into Baltimore really late, checked into the team's training camp headquarters and noticed a note attached to my door. It simply read, "See Coach in the morning."

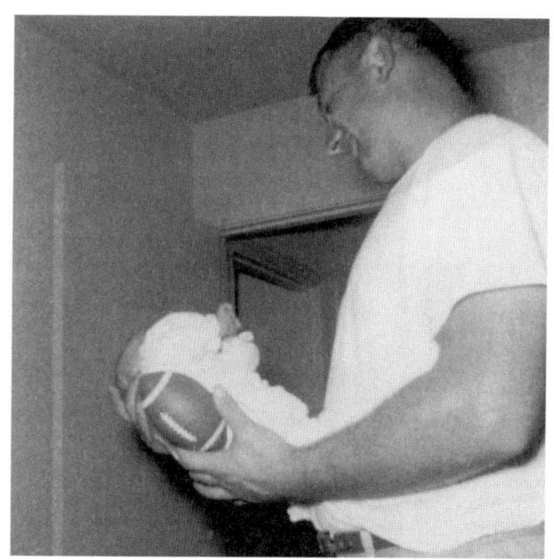

He's got the whole world in his hands.

I woke up around six o'clock (I've always been an early riser), and after a shower and a bite to eat, I went straight to Coach Ewbank's office. I walked in, sat down, and could tell immediately that something was up. He told me I was a good football player, and that I would become a really, really good one before I was through. But…

Coach Ewbank said the Colts needed a linebacker in the worst way and that he had no choice but to trade me to the Green Bay Packers. Coach Ewbank informed me that, while he liked my potential, he needed another linebacker. So the Colts traded me to Green Bay for Marv Matuszak.

I was speechless. I didn't know what to say. I just blinked, and sat there, and tried to sort out the million things that were going through my mind. Then, I got up, thanked Coach Ewbank, shook his hand, and was off to Green Bay. I didn't understand why he couldn't have told me this before I got in the car and drove eighteen hours. I was pissed off.

The Colts were the defending World Champions, a team dotted with Hall of Fame players, and we had every intention of successfully defending that title.

The Packers? They were coming off a dismal 1-10-1 season, in which, they placed sixth in the Western Conference. It led to Ray "Scooter" McLean's dismissal and Coach Vince Lombardi's arrival. Lombardi had never held a head coaching job in the NFL, and I hadn't paid any attention to him up to that point. He was an assistant coach under Jim Lee Howell with the New York Giants, the team we defeated 13-10 in 1958 World Championship, the first sudden death overtime game in National Football League history. To this day, along with the Ice Bowl, it is considered one of the NFL's greatest games.

I was on my way to a losing team with a rookie head coach. Hell, the last time we played the Packers it was at Baltimore in November of '58, and we blasted them 56-0. I knew the Packers weren't very good, but I also knew that their new Head Coach, Vincent T. Lombardi, believed he could build a winner.

Now, I was going to be on the Packers' sideline. Maybe I wasn't the smartest guy around, but after dealing with the initial disappointment, I didn't think it was such a bad thing. Hell, I didn't think it was too bad at all. Sure, I was disappointed because the Colts traded me, but I tried to look on the bright side. I learned at a young age from my mother to view adversity as an opportunity to learn and improve. That's what I have been doing my whole life. I decided to turn what appeared to be a negative experience into a positive opportunity. I would survive and be happy, and I would make the most of this opportunity. This attitude had been instrumental in enduring all of life's changes to that point, and this situation would be no different.

I was going home. I was a Wisconsin native, born and bred in Altoona, home of the Railroaders. I was going to be playing for the Green Bay Packers, the team I idolized and dreamed about growing up in that tiny town in northeast Wisconsin. All I ever wanted when I was a kid was maybe, just maybe, a chance to WATCH a Packers game at City Stadium. How faraway it seemed. How wonderful it would be.

On the drive from Baltimore back to Wisconsin, I thought, "This is going to be my home. Please, God, no more. I've been around. I've done it. I've paid the price. Let me be here and stay here." By the time I hit the Maryland state line, I had adjusted my perspective, finding all the good in what started out as a major disappointment. I was the happiest guy in the world. I was going to see my wife, Susan, and our beautiful family that included a newborn son. I was going to be playing for the team I loved while I was growing up. I wasn't going to be a loser. I was coming home. It was just a matter of rearranging my attitude and my expectations, and it was going to be all right. In fact, it was going to be fantastic.

Left to right: Bob Skoronski, Jerry Kramer, Tom Moore and Forrest Gr

I loved Wisconsin. I knew the Packers had their work ahead of them, but I was excited by the idea of playing for them. Also, in the back of my mind, I thought about the Packers' offensive line. They had Bob Skoronski at left tackle, Jim Ringo at center, Jerry Kramer at right guard and Forrest Gregg at right tackle. And now they had a feisty left guard named Fuzzy Thurston.

I liked our potential, and I loved the fact that I was coming home.

ROAD TO THE NFL

1951-52 Valparaiso **(freshman)**
Thurston played at guard on the basketball team, discus and shot put in track and field, wrestled.

1952-53 Valparaiso **(sophomore)**
Thurston played at guard on the basketball team, discus and shot put in track and field, wrestled.

1953 Valparaiso **(sophomore, 2nd semester)**
Thurston was approached by Walt Reiner, a football assistant coach, and asked if he would be interested in playing football. Thurston agreed to play in Valparaiso's spring game. He played at defensive end and was impressive.

1953 Valparaiso **(summer before junior year)**
Reiner gave Thurston a crash course in Football to prepare him for the fall football season.

1953-54 Valparaiso **(junior)**
Thurston played at left tackle for Valparaiso football team and received all-conference recognition.

1954-55 Valparaiso **(senior)**
Thurston played at left tackle for Valparaiso football team and again received all-conference recognition. NFL scouts began to take notice of Thurston.

1955-56 Valparaiso **(fifth-year senior)**
At Reiner's urging, Thurston returned for a fifth year (one final year of football eligibility) and became the first offensive lineman to be named Most Valuable Player.

1956 Philadelphia Eagles
The Eagles selected Thurston in the fourth round of the NFL draft.

1956-58 United States Army

Thurston played in three exhibition games, was released by the Eagles, and was drafted by the US Army. He served 21 months military duty, much of which was spent playing football for the Army.

1958 Chicago Bears

Upon recommendation from Bears receiver Harlon Hill, Chicago owner George "Papa Bear" Halas signed Thurston to a contract. Thurston played three exhibition games before being traded to Philadelphia.

1958 Philadelphia Eagles

Thurston played the Eagles' final exhibition game, but was released four days before the regular-season opener.

1958 Winnipeg Blue Bombers

Head Coach Bud Grant informed Thurston that the Baltimore Colts wanted to sign him to their taxi squad. Thurston signed with the Colts.

1958 Baltimore Colts

Thurston was placed on the Colts' active roster with six games to play.

1958 Baltimore Colts

The Colts defeated the New York Giants, 23-17, in sudden death overtime. It is considered one of the NFL's all-time greatest games. Thurston played on special teams and became a World Champion.

1959 Green Bay Packers

Thurston drove from Wisconsin to Baltimore to report for training camp. Colts coach Weeb Ewbank informed him he had been traded to the Packers for linebacker Marv Matuszak. Thurston drove to Green Bay, met Coach Lombardi, and the rest is history.

"You played your hearts out. I am proud of you. We should have won the game ... when we return to another championship game, we will never lose."

Chapter 4
World Championships and Super Bowls

So much has been written and said about Coach Vince Lombardi's comment, "Winning isn't everything. It's the only thing." I can tell you firsthand that he meant the will to win is everything.

Coach Lombardi emphatically and emotionally delivered that message inside a gloomy visitor's locker room at Philadelphia's Franklin Field. The Eagles had beaten us, 17-13, in the 1960 NFL Championship Game. We were heartbroken.

It was the Packers' first championship game in 16 years, and we felt like we had failed our great fans. We had taken a 13-10 lead in the fourth quarter on Bart Starr's 7-yard touchdown pass to Max McGee, but we couldn't hold it because all three phases of the game, offense, defense and special teams, failed to sew up the victory.

We gave up a 58-yard kickoff return to the Eagles' Ted Dean after we scored the go-ahead touchdown. That led to Dean's 5-yard touchdown run that gave Philadelphia a 17-13 lead with five minutes to play.

When the offense took the field, I was certain we were going to drive down the field and score the game-winning touchdown. We got to the Eagles' 22-yard line, and Starr completed a short pass to Jim Taylor out of the backfield, but Chuck Bednarik wrestled him to the ground at the Philadelphia 8 as time expired.

The ending was so sudden, and I felt so empty and so sad, because I couldn't believe we didn't get it done. I don't think we looked at each other when the game ended. We just shuffled off the field and into the locker room with our heads down. It was like we were in a daze.

After what seemed like an eternity, Coach Lombardi walked into the locker room and stood in front of the players. Then, he cleared his throat and addressed the team, "You played your hearts out. I'm proud of you. We should've won the game, but we didn't. I'm going to tell you today that we'll be back, real soon, for another championship game. And let me also tell you that when we return to another championship game, we will never lose it."

Coach Lombardi repeated himself several times until he had tears in his eyes. That was the first of six NFL Championship Games and two Super Bowls under Coach Lombardi, and it was the only championship game we ever lost. It was a difficult lesson, but an important lesson for us to learn.

We didn't focus on winning or losing all those years. We focused on concentrating, executing and trying to give it our best. We had talent, which helped, but we didn't dwell on the outcome of upcoming games.

We figured if we took care of business, and we kept alive that will to win, everything else would take care of itself.

We put that philosophy to the test the following season, and the results were undeniable. We finished 11-3 to win the Western Conference Title, and earned the right to play the New York Giants in the 1961 NFL Championship Game.

We defeated the Giants, 37-0, at Lambeau Field and it wasn't that close. To this day, I believe it represents one of the greatest wins in NFL playoff history.

1961 Championship Game vs. the New York Giants. Vince Lombardi and assistant coach Bill Austin on the sidelines first title game ever played on what would become known as the legendary "frozen tu

#24 Safety Willie Wood pulls down one of the four interceptions Green Bay had against the Giants in the 1961 Championship Game.

Our defense intercepted four passes, recovered a fumble and limited the Giants to six first downs. It was 24-0 at halftime and Coach Lombardi said, "We're playing with a lot of effort, and it's all good, so if we continue the way we're going there is no way they're going to beat us."

Tight end Ron Kramer was phenomenal. He caught two touchdown passes from Bart and showed why he is the last of Michigan's athletes to win nine letters. He was a better athlete than a lot of people gave him credit for, but we knew his importance to both the running game and the passing game in our offense.

The Packers make history with the first shutout in an NFL Championship Game.

Before the game, several of the New York writers predicted that Giants' quarterback, Y.A. Tittle, was going to turn "Titletown, USA," into "Tittle-Town." Tittle completed just six of 20 passes for 64 yards before being replaced by Charley Conerly, who fared no better, late in the first half.

Red Smith, a Green Bay native, was the sports columnist for the New York Herald-Tribune. After the game, he wrote, "Not even the unsightly score of 37 to 0 – first shutout in 12 title play-offs – reflects the shocking abuse to which the Giants were subjected. They skidded and floundered on the frozen turf."

Red Smith had a better day than the Giants and their coach, Allie Sherman. The Giants were no slouches, and they had great players, such as Jim Katcabage, Dick Modzelewski, Rosey Grier, Andy Robustelli, Alex Webster,

Kyle Rote and Sam Huff. The Giants were very good, but we were that much better.

We rushed for 181 yards even though the Giants occasionally deployed a five-man defensive front, and, when we couldn't run, Bart threw it right on the money. He completed 10 of 17 passes, including three touchdowns. Of his 10 completions, eight went for first downs, and he didn't throw a single interception.

As much as the loss to Philadelphia in the 1960 NFL Championship fueled our will to win, the victory over the New York Giants in the 1961 NFL Championship set the stage for a decade of dominance.

No matter where I went in the country, people would ask, "How did you murder the Giants?" It wasn't that people didn't think we could beat the Giants. It was that they didn't think we could blow them out by 37 points and shut them out in the process.

What some people suspected, and we thought to be true, was that it was only the beginning. In my opinion, the 1962 team was the greatest I ever played on. Coach Lombardi was developing a team. We were all pretty young and had also been together for three years. We were quick, fast, strong and smart. We were in our prime. That 1962 team may be the best overall team in Packers history.

We lost one player, Em Tunnell, from the '61 team; he was a backup in the defensive secondary. We also got Paul Hornung, Ray Nitschke and Boyd Dowler back full-time after being in and out of the lineup in '61 because of Army obligations.

By 1962, the cornerstones of Coach Lombardi's philosophy had taken root. Repetition, constant repetition, was ingrained in us. If you ran the sweep 50 times a day for three years, you got to know what you were doing. We were at the height of the Packers' sweep. I don't know if it got any better after that. It stayed really good during the next four or five years, but it was never better than in 1962.

We had players with great size, for those days, plus great knowledge and a lot of time spent working together. When Jerry and I turned the corner, Ron Kramer had either wiped out the linebacker or he had him out of position. Once in a while, a defender would slip through from the off side and make the tackle, but that was a great once in a while.

When the sweep worked we were almost always unstoppable. It helped that we had great talent at the receiver position. Max McGee and Boyd Dowler, our receivers, had excellent size, tremendous know-how and great hands. Their greatest asset was getting open and catching the football. I know that sounds simple, but it was true.

I don't remember them dropping anything. Some passes were behind them, or too high, or too low, but the ones they could catch, they caught. It was unbelievable. They also prevented interceptions because they were so tall they could knock down bad passes.

Packers Wide Receiver Boyd Dowler

Boyd was 6-foot-5, 225 pounds. Max was 6-foot-3, 205 pounds. Ron Kramer was 6-foot-4, 260 pounds and Paul Hornung was 6 foot 3, 215 pounds. They all had great size for receivers and they used it to their advantage. Ron Kramer had the biggest hands of anyone I ever saw, and without a doubt, he was the best blocking tight end of all-time.

Max and Boyd both caught 49 passes in 1962. You couldn't double-team anybody. You had to play them man-to-man. Ron Kramer caught 37 passes with seven touchdowns. Max (three) and Boyd (two) combined for five touchdowns.

Max wasn't the fastest receiver, but speed doesn't get you open all the time. He was one of the all-time great receivers at getting open when nobody else could. He had a great sense for knowing what the defensive back was trying to take away, and then doing the opposite to counteract it.

Boyd was so tall and so quick that he could catch anything, even if it was thrown high. He was effective in all phases of the passing game. He could do a quick turn-in, go over the middle or catch the long pass up the sideline.

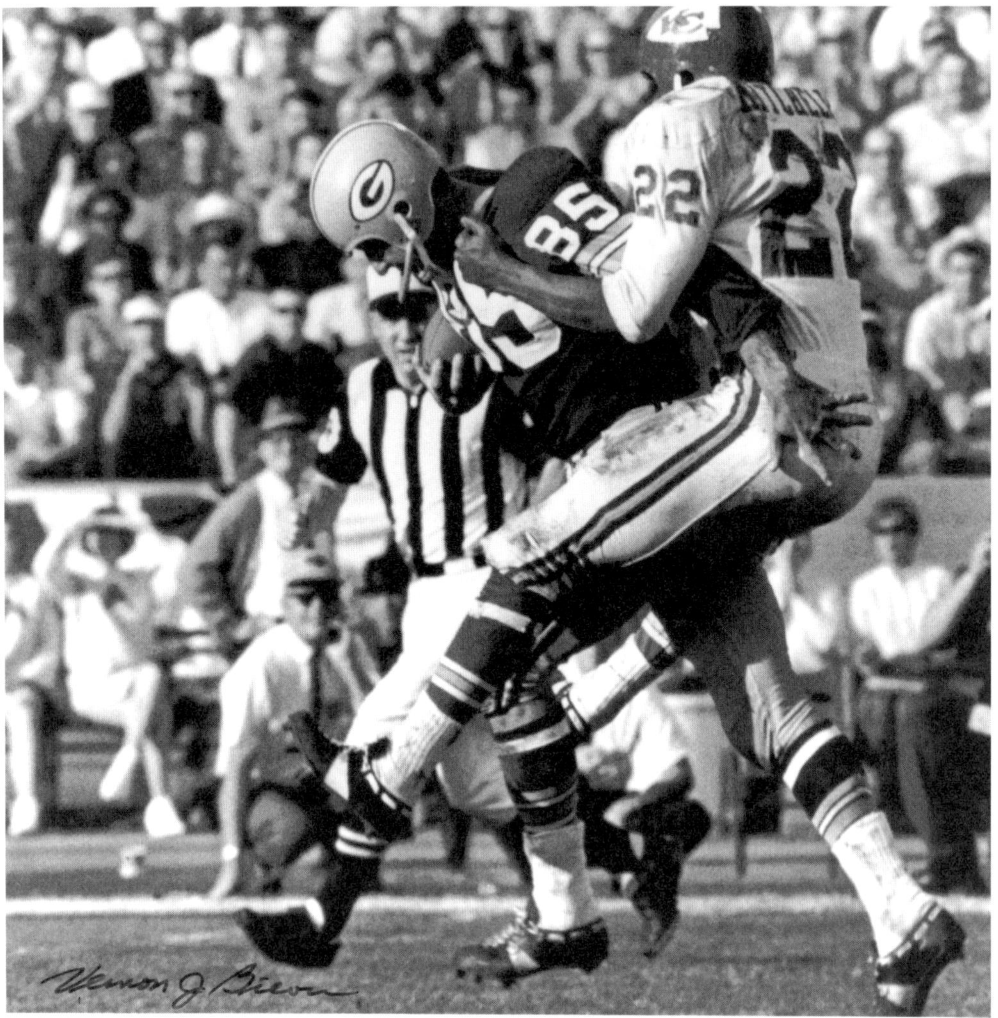

Wide Receiver Max McGee - Super Bowl I vs the Kansas City Chiefs.

Boyd and Max also were such great athletes that they handled the punting. Boyd punted 36 times for a 43.1-yard average, and Max had 14 punts for a 35.4-yard average. We didn't need an extra roster spot for a punter because we had them.

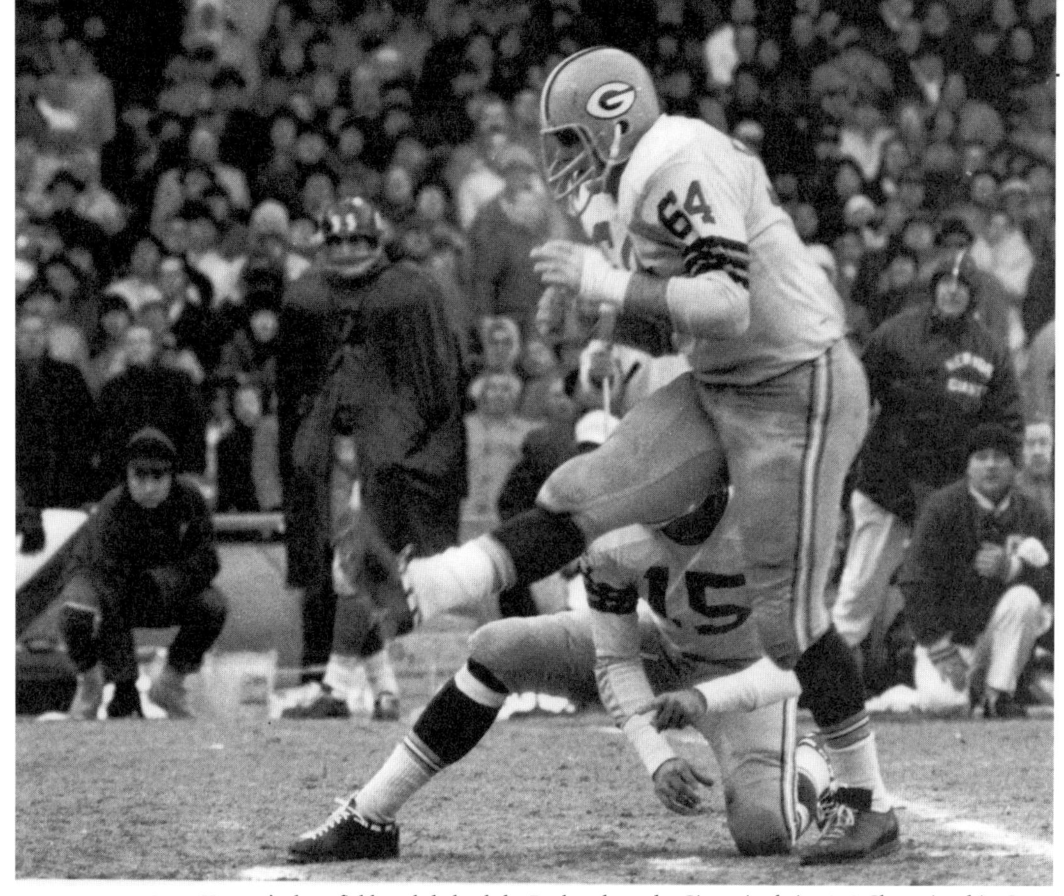

Jerry Kramer's three field goals helped the Packers beat the Giants in their 1962 Championship Game.

It was the same for field goals and kickoffs. Jerry Kramer was 9 for 11 on field goals, and Paul Hornung was 6 for 10. These days, all NFL teams have kickers and punters. We had four great all-purpose athletes in Dowler, McGee, Kramer and Hornung - position players that could also kick.

If Max and Boyd had a weakness, it was their blocking. Boyd was bad at it, and Max wouldn't attempt it. We kidded them all the time. Boyd would try to block downfield, and he gave great effort, but he didn't have a knack for it. Max wanted nothing to do with it. He would get in the way and try to screen defenders, but he wasn't going to leave the ground for anything.

It didn't matter because most of the time we had it covered anyway. We had a pair of Hall of Fame running backs in Hornung and Taylor, and we had a solid offensive line paving the way.

Jim Taylor was a straight-ahead power back. He had a tremendous blend of quickness and strength, and he loved to run over tacklers. I think he enjoyed running into them, too. He would hit a tackler, bounce off, and go for more yards. He was very quiet, not outgoing at all. He let his running do the talking.

Fuzzy clears the way for Fullback Jimmy Taylor

Jim, Jerry and I would go out to dinner together on the road. It was just the three of us, and we would talk football about 90 percent of the time. It became a tradition, and one that Jim really liked, I think, because he never paid for anything. We would have a beer with our meal, and Jerry would pay for it. We would have another beer, and I would pay for it. Then, when it came time for the third beer, before we went back to the hotel, Jim would say, "Boys, I've had enough, but you go ahead." Jerry and I would wink at each other and call him cheap. Jim didn't mind. He called it being conservative.

Paul was our other Hall of Fame back. He was brilliant. Smart. He used blockers better than anybody I ever played with. When he saw the opening he would put on a burst of speed and hit the hole full blast. He was the best at it. Paul would break more runs than any back because of his vision and his patience.

Tom Moore was the backup running back, and he played for six seasons. He was very good, and very dependable when he got a chance, but he couldn't crack the starting lineup with Hornung and Taylor ahead of him.

We worked on the running game constantly, and in 1962 we averaged 175 yards rushing per game, which is amazing to me. We had great backs, but we also had a great offensive line and a great scheme.

Bob Skoronski, our captain, was one of the team's leaders. He never made a mistake and he always got the job done. In nine seasons I never once had to worry about the defensive end. I just knew he would take care of him. He also had a great attitude, and it made coming to work that much more fun.

Jim Ringo, our center, was the smartest and quickest center I played with. He did it with quickness. He had to keep the tackle or the middle linebacker from chasing the play, and he was quick enough to get it done.

Very few could, but he did.

Jerry Kramer was one of the best right guards that ever played the game. He was quick, fast, and if he had a weakness it was pass blocking, but he always got the job done.

What can I say about Forrest Gregg? Coach Lombardi said he was the best player he ever coached. Do you argue with Coach Lombardi? No. So, he was the best.

As a group we really cared for each other. We wanted to win games, and we wanted each other to play well and receive honors each week. We were a team, a unit, and as a group, I think we were the greatest offensive line in NFL history.

Whenever anyone asked which was better, the offense or the defense, the guys on offense would say, "We have the greatest defense in the league." And the guys on defense would say, "We

Middle Linebacker Ray Nitschke. Nitschke was named MVP in the Packers' 1962 Championship rematch against New York.

have the greatest offense in the league." We were a team. If we lost, the offense felt it was because we didn't score enough points, and the defense felt like it had given up too many. Again, that sounds simple, but it was the attitude Coach Lombardi instilled, and the attitude that we played with.

That said, we really did have a great defense. I loved it when we'd watch them, and it was great to see the way they played. Willie Davis, our co-captain along with Bob Skoronski, did everything you could expect from a great defensive end. He would rush the passer, he would stuff the run, he was quick, and he was strong. He had a great attitude, which made him a great leader.

Henry Jordan was amazing. What more can I say?

Dave "Hog" Hanner, our other tackle, was powerful. He wasn't a great pass rusher, but man he could clog the middle of the line.

Lionel Aldridge always gave his best effort. He had a lot of personal problems through the years, but he always played well, and he was really good in '62.

Dan Currie, one of the outside linebackers, was a fireplug. He did a lot of talking, and he backed up most of it. He was a good player and a good friend.

Bill Forester, the other outside linebacker, was a surprise. He didn't talk much, but he could play and was very intelligent.

There was nobody better than Ray Nitschke at middle linebacker. Some people say the Bears' Dick Butkus was better. I say flip a coin.

Cornerback Herb Adderley

Herb Adderley was the best cornerback that ever played. He was outstanding in every phase of the game. He went an entire season without giving up a touchdown, and he was big enough and physical enough to tackle anyone in the open field. He also returned kickoffs and averaged almost 28 yards a return in '62. He returned one kickoff 103 yards for a touchdown, and it was the difference in a 9-7 win over Detroit.

Jesse Whittenton was my roommate and my good friend. He had to be pretty darn good because I don't remember him getting beat very often, and nobody ever wanted to throw it in Herb's direction.

Hank Gremminger, one of our safeties, was a lot like Jesse. You never heard much about him, but nobody ever beat him, either. He was a hardnosed tackler and he loved to play the game.

Willie Wood was a great safety. He is one of only 6 walk-on players ever inducted to the Pro Football Hall of Fame. He was 5' 10" and 160 pounds soaking wet, but he knocked the hell out of everybody he played against. That's why he can't walk today. He was a picture-perfect tackler, and he was so agile on punt returns, too. He would fair catch only when he absolutely had to, and he had more than his share of big returns and big interceptions.

We knew our defense was great. We knew that if we

Green Bay's second straight World Title. 1962 Championship Game at Yankee Stadium.

scored two touchdowns we had a great chance to win. That year we finished 13-1. We outscored our opponents 415 points to 148 points, which equates to a 28-10 win average for the 14 games.

We played the Giants for the 1962 NFL Championship at Yankee Stadium. It was the rematch from the previous year, and it was terribly cold. It felt colder in New York than Green Bay, about 13 degrees without the wind chill, and there were 40 mph winds.

Jimmy Taylor and Sam Huff went after each other from the start. Jimmy set a playoff record by rushing 31 times, and he finished with a hard-fought 85 yards. When Huff wasn't chasing Taylor, Ray Nitschke was tackling every Giant in sight. Ray ended up being named the game's Most Valuable Player, and we came away with a 16-7 win. It was our third straight appearance in the NFL Championship Game, and our second straight World Title.

We might have won a third straight title in '63 if fate hadn't intervened. We were 11-2-1 and finished in second place in the Western Conference. The Chicago Bears went 11-1-2 to capture the conference title, but first place wasn't decided until the final game of the season. The Bears and Lions met in the season finale, and we needed Detroit to win in order to face the Giants a third straight time in the NFL Championship Game.

Dinah Washington, the famous singer and wife of the Lions' Dick "Night Train" Lane, died just a few days before the Lions-Bears game. "Night Train" Lane, one of the best defensive backs in the game, didn't play because of his wife's death. The Bears threw the ball all over the field, which wouldn't have happened if he was playing, and they ended up winning the game. The Lions' record was 5-8-1 that year, but they were better than that. Our tie came against the Lions, 13-13, in Detroit on Thanksgiving Day.

That was the 13th and final time the Packers and Lions played in Detroit on Thanksgiving Day. Coach Lombardi didn't like the idea of having to travel to Detroit and play a road game against a conference rival on three days' rest. He didn't think it was fair, and the series' record proves it. The Packers were 3-9-1 in Thanksgiving Day games at Detroit before the NFL discontinued the tradition. That tie cost us a chance to play in the 1963 World Championship game, and Coach Lombardi had no intention of risking a repeat in the future.

In fairness to the Bears, they beat us twice that season, 10-3 in the season opener in Green Bay, and 26-7 at Chicago in November. People can say that we had our chance, and they would be right, but it would've been nice to get another chance at the Giants.

There were a lot of reasons we won five World Championships and two Super Bowls, and those reasons include several intangibles.

I am always amazed that we were able to stay healthy for so long. I didn't pay attention to other teams' injuries, but it seemed like we were lucky. I know I was very fortunate. I had a couple of sprained ankles and a separated right shoulder, but that was the extent of my injuries. For all the times we ran the sweep, Jerry Kramer and I never had knee problems, and our knees are still pretty good to this day.

Jerry had more injuries than anybody on the team, but he also was able to bounce back each time. In 1960, he sustained a torn retina, but kept playing. He said it wasn't the pain that bothered him, so much as all those flickering little lights. He had surgery in January of 1961 at General Hospital in Madison, and he was back at right guard the next season.

Jerry was injured the following season when he was hammered on a kick return. He separated two bones and stretched ligaments in his left ankle. He was on crutches for the final eight games of the season.

Once again, he came back strong the following season and never missed a beat. He also required surgery to remove a large splinter of wood from his stomach, but that wasn't a football-related injury. He had been skewered when he fell on a piece of wood as child growing up in Idaho. True to form, he came back from that surgery, too.

We almost had a catastrophic injury during practice when a steel observation tower collapsed. It hit Ray Nitschke on the head, flattened him, and Coach Lombardi began shouting, "Who is it? Who got hit?"

"Nitschke," Bart Starr replied.

"Oh," Coach Lombardi said. "Let's get back to practice."

Ray loved telling that story because he said Coach Lombardi always knew nothing could hurt his head.

I am often asked if we could have survived free agency, and if we would have lost players to other teams willing to pay more. Yes, we would have. Who wouldn't go to another team for $4 million more? Money talks, especially when it's such a huge amount. But I don't agree with a guy signing a five-year contract and then threatening to hold out for more money when he's still got 3 years left on the original contract.

If any of our guys had signed a five-year deal, let's say, they wouldn't have asked Coach Lombardi for more money until it was time. I truly believe that. The NFL is the best game going, by far, in professional sports, but the increase in money has made the game worse to a degree. It doesn't upset me when a guy wants a lot of money, but once he has signed a contract, he should honor the agreement until it's time to renegotiate.

I realize today's players are concerned about being injured, and there is a lot of money at stake, but the owners need to put their foot down. The threat of holdouts detracts from the game, and it almost always ends badly for the player, the team, or both.

Conditioning is another aspect of the game that has changed tremendously. I never lifted weights until my last year, and I think injuries occur because today's players are simply too big for their frames. They weigh 320 or 330, and they should be weighing 250 or 260. It puts too much stress on their bodies, and when they get hit, they explode. I don't know if this is true, but it seems to make sense. If we had weight training when we played, you could add another 30 or 35 pounds to every player, especially the linemen. I think you would have seen a lot more injuries then, too.

There also has been a lot of talk about steroids and human growth hormones and that sort of thing, but we never had steroids when I was playing. If we did, I never knew about it, and nobody ever brought it around me. There may have been players that smoked marijuana, but again, my feeling was that whatever anyone wanted to do was their business. I just didn't want them to bring it around me because I wanted nothing to do with it.

I preferred alcohol, of course, but even then we tried to observe guidelines and use some common sense. Coach Lombardi didn't have a rule that we couldn't drink, or that we couldn't drink the night before games, but he didn't have to. We wanted to perform at our best and he trusted us.

Thurston, McGee and Adderley at Matteo's restaurant in Los Angeles the night before Super Bowl I.

I remember the night before Super Bowl I in Los Angeles. Herb Adderley and his wife, Max McGee and a girlfriend, and Sue and I were out at a fancy restaurant. We were having drinks before dinner at a circular booth. All of a sudden Tony Canadeo, the Packers' Hall of Fame running back, came in and said, "If you've got any drinks get rid of them because Vince is coming in."

Out of all the restaurants in Los Angeles, we ended up at the same one. What are the chances of that?

The wives and girlfriends kept their drinks, but I pushed my martini in front of Sue, or I threw it on the floor, I can't remember which. It wasn't so much that we couldn't drink, but that I lost the drink out of respect for Coach Lombardi. I also think he sent Tony in ahead of him in order to avoid embarrassing any of his players.

Those were simpler times, but I think people treated each other with more respect, at least for the most part. We were a team, we cared what each other thought, and we cared about each other's feelings. There wasn't free agency then, so we were able to keep that team together a long, long time. I have to admit it's easier to stay together when you're winning. It never entered my mind to play for anyone else, and I think my teammates felt the same. We had so many good times, and so many memorable victories.

The 1965 Western Conference Championship Game was a classic. It was the Packers' first overtime game in their history, and we won 13-10 at Lambeau Field on Don Chandler's 25-yard field goal at 13:39 of sudden death.

That game is memorable because Chandler's first field goal, a 22-yarder with 1:58 to play in regulation, still remains controversial. Some say it sailed right, but I had twenty-twenty vision, and I could see that it was good. That kick forced the league to extend the goal posts the next season. To this day, Colts fans swear the kick was wide right.

The 1965 NFL Championship, again at Lambeau Field, was another memorable game for several reasons. We defeated the Cleveland Browns, 23-12, on a day when four inches of snow softened up the field. It was probably the greatest running attack ever seen in a championship game. We

Don Chandler kicks the winning field goal in sudden death overtime to clinch the 1965 Western Conference Championship.

won our third championship in five years by rushing for 201 yards against the Browns. Taylor had 27 carries for 96 yards, and Hornung had 18 carries for 105 yards. We were so confident going into the game because we knew the muddy, slippery surface was going to be a huge advantage. We ran the ball down their throats. The Browns weren't so fortunate, though. Jim Brown, the great running back, finished with just 50 yards. It was the final game of his illustrious career.

The 1966 NFL Championship game, a 34-27 thriller against Dallas in the Cotton Bowl, was one of the toughest games I ever played. I had to go against Bob Lilly, the Cowboys' great defensive tackle, and he was all over the place. When Tom Brown intercepted the Cowboys' Don Meredith in the back of the end zone with 28 seconds to play, I was just happy that we had the lead. It was such a back-and-forth game, and Bart played terrific. He had four touchdown passes that day.

That victory set up a Super Bowl I match-up against Kansas City at the Memorial Coliseum in Los Angeles. The biggest challenge we faced in the week leading up to the game was that we were heavy favorites and knew we were better than Kansas City. In an effort to keep us from believing our press clippings, Coach Lombardi rode us very hard in practice.

The week was very exciting, not just for me, but for my family as well. It was my wife's first trip to Los Angeles, and her parents joined us in California. They were so nervous before the game. I think Sue was the first person in the stands on game day. As exciting as it was, it was also very scary. I found myself thinking about how bad it would be if we lost. I think it affected me more than my teammates, because I had to play against Buck Buchanon, one of the best defensive tackles in history.

A nervous Sue Thurston and her pa
in the stands at Super Bc

Super Bowl I was an amazing experience and, as predicted, we went on to beat the Chiefs, 35-10, to protect the NFL's honor against the AFL and to go down in the history books as the winner of the first Super Bowl. I still enjoy reading some of the newspaper accounts of that game.

Dick Connor of the Denver Post wrote: "The Packers methodically, mercilessly, convincingly whipped the Chiefs. A crowd of 63,036 – 30,000 less than capacity – witnessed the destruction of AFL hopes that the junior circuit could, in one game, achieve equality with the proud NFL."

Joe Falls of the Detroit Free-Press wrote: "It was such fun in the Green Bay dressing room. Nobody even paid attention to the sign over the door: Guard Your Valuables. The Packers had done that on the field." We sure had.

I also felt good about the way I played against the Chiefs' Buck Buchanan. The massive defensive tackle had received rave reviews leading up to the game. Afterward, after I throttled him for most of the game, there wasn't much else to be written. I had done my talking on the field and in the trenches. I was so happy when I walked out of the locker room to greet my family after playing such a great game. The celebration started in Los Angeles that night and continued in Las Vegas the next day. What a weekend!

Of course, the Ice Bowl capped the next season, and our 21-17 win against Dallas on Dec. 31, 1967, remains one of the NFL's greatest games ever. When anyone asks what I remember about the game, I say, "It was cold. Brutally cold." I ran down to cover a kickoff, and I barely touched one of

Bart Starr's quarterback sneak in the legendary Ice Bowl, still considered one of the greatest games in NFL history.

the Cowboys' blockers, but when he fell on the turf it sounded like he'd fallen out of a six-story building and landed on concrete. It was that cold.

I was on special teams at that stage of my career. A young, talented player by the name of Gale Gillingham had taken over my job at left guard. I liked Gale, he could play, and I accepted that without a word. I began playing special teams with the 1958 World Champion Baltimore Colts, and I ended playing special teams with the Super Bowl II champion Green Bay Packers.

I remember, as a rookie with the Colts, receiving compliments from some of the veterans because I played so hard on special teams and never complained. I also remember receiving letters of admiration from Packers fans when I played so hard on special teams and never complained, at the end of my career.

We went on to defeat the Oakland Raiders 33-14 at the Orange Bowl in Super Bowl II. That was the final game of my career. It was also the final game that Vince Lombardi coached for the Green Bay Packers. I didn't know it at the time, but this was an end of an era, for me, my teammates, Coach Lombardi and the entire Packers organization. Our lives would never be the same.

In looking back, it bothers me that Super Bowls tend to overshadow the NFL Championship games that came before. I feel bad for my teammates that played so hard and so well in the early 1960s and have been seemingly forgotten.

The only thing the press talks about is the Super Bowls, and that's not fair. They should also talk about the teams and the men that won world championships before the Super Bowl was a concept. Fortunately, I'm part of both, so I don't get slighted. But, guys like Jim Ringo, Ron Kramer, Dave Hanner, Bill Forester, Hank Gremminger, Jesse Whittenton, Dan Currie, Bill Quinlan and others deserve better.

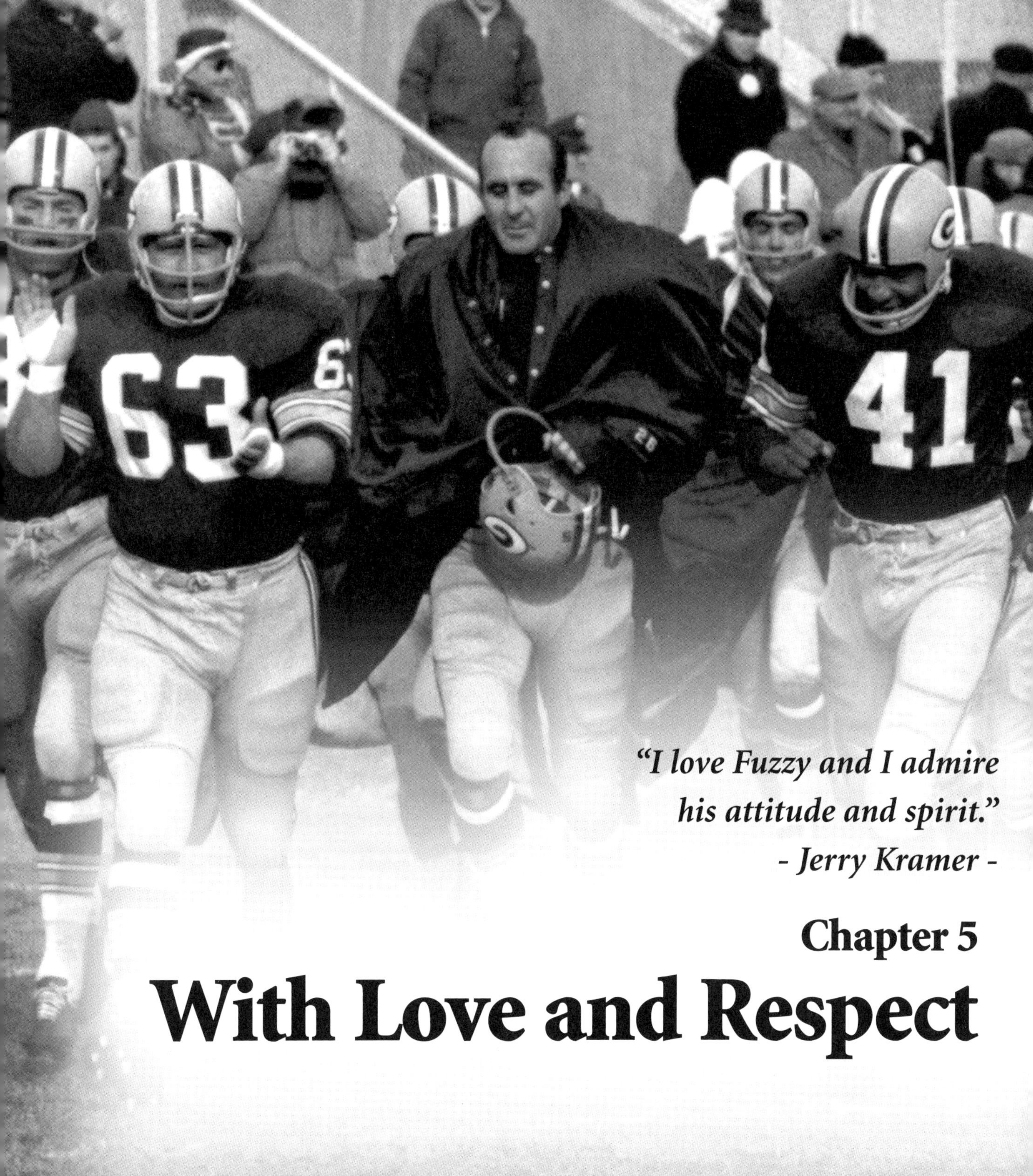

"I love Fuzzy and I admire his attitude and spirit."

- Jerry Kramer -

Chapter 5

With Love and Respect

Vince Lombardi once said, "Teamwork is what the Green Bay Packers were all about. They didn't do it for individual glory. They did it because they loved one another." There is no statement more accurate in defining Lombardi's Green Bay Packers.

In the history of sports, it is extremely rare for teammates to have the love and respect that Lombardi's Packers had for each other. It's amazing to see men that are apart for years get back together and interact like time stood still. It's truly special. Lombardi's Packers remain as close today as they were in the 1960's. It is a bond that will last a lifetime.

How did these players build such a strong and unique bond? Maybe it was because of the nucleus of Lombardi's teams played together for so long. Perhaps it was just the common goal they shared - the will to win. Or maybe they were bound together by their mutual love, hatred and respect for

Coach Lombardi. Together, they endured his wrath and celebrated their success. Whatever the reasons, they share a feeling of love and respect for each other.

Through adversity and advantage alike, it's certain they share love and respect for their teammate, their friend, Fuzzy Thurston.

Fuzzy always had a tremendous amount of respect, admiration and affection for his teammates, and still does. It's clear his teammates felt the same, and still do. Here are their thoughts about what it was like to be Fuzzy Thurston's friend and teammate:

BOB SKORONSKI
TACKLE
1956, 1959-68

When you think about that entire team, Fuzzy was the only true Wisconsin guy. He was from Wisconsin, he loved everything about Wisconsin, and he loved the Green Bay Packers, the Milwaukee Brewers, and the Wisconsin Badgers. It was so right for him to have the career he had because Fuzzy and Wisconsin just go together. All the players loved Wisconsin, of course, but Fuzzy's love was special. I saw it. I could feel it. He grew up in Wisconsin, he played for the Packers and he stayed in Wisconsin.

As a player, I would call him the most reliable guy we had from the standpoint of always being able to do the job. His consistency was absolutely amazing. There might've been someone that did something flashier or more eye-catching, but Fuzzy was there all day, all the time. He got it done all the time. He played across from a lot of great football players, and he was extremely reliable.

When I look at Paul Hornung and the scoring record, I think of the great blocks Fuzzy delivered for him time and time again. Fuzzy was also great at talking during the game. He would get the Colts' Big Daddy Lipscomb talking about having a cold beer, or the wife and kids, or what it was like playing together in Baltimore. It was a part of the game strategy. Fuzzy got them thinking about everything but their assignments.

Fuzzy was always very positive. One of the tough deals in those days was watching film after a game. We all had our mistakes in games, and we would sit in our chairs with fear waiting for the part of the film where we didn't do as well as we should have. Coach Lombardi would keep going back and forth, back and forth, on the same play, sometimes 10 or 15 times. Finally, Fuzzy would jump up and say, "I know it coach. I know I screwed up." He took all the tension from the air watching the film that day.

I've been asked a lot of questions about who belongs in what Hall of Fame, and I always say that if somebody's going in, Fuzzy has to be included. I don't say that because I played with him. I say it because I'm a little bit of a statistician. I kept a record of every guy's performance, and when you talk about consistency, Fuzzy had it. Here, we have this entire offensive backfield in the Pro Football Hall of Fame, but does anybody ever wonder how they got voted in there?

DAVE ROBINSON
OUTSIDE LINEBACKER
1963-72

When I came in as a first-round draft choice in1963, I was excited because I was going to the Green Bay Packers, the World Champions, the best team in the NFL. Vince Lombardi had a mild form of hazing, and some of the veterans were pretty rough on rookies, but Fuzzy was just the opposite. He was the man. He was No. 63, the left guard, the man that paved the way on the sweep. Well, the rookies had to sing for their supper during training camp. Whenever one of us was hurting, or couldn't remember the words to a song, or there was a little lull in the action, Fuzzy would break out in a chorus of, "He's got the whole world, in his hands." He would save the day for us. We took a big liking to Fuzzy right away.

Fuzzy was also color blind. I could talk about it, but it doesn't sound the same today as it did in 1963. The Civil Rights Act wasn't voted into action until 1964, and it didn't take effect until 1968. There were no black linebackers in the NFL. There were a few in the AFL, but not the NFL, and it was very uncommon in 1963 for a team to draft a black player with a first-round pick. That caused a lot of people that were "football knowledgeable" to say Vince was wasting draft choices on black guys. Fuzzy understood that Coach Lombardi was doing it for the good of the team. He smoothed the waters for us. He was a negotiator, a mediator, a friend, and he was one of the guys that the black players gravitated toward. He owned a restaurant down there in Neenah-Menasha, and in those days, not every restaurant wanted black guys coming in. Fuzzy made sure we got equal billing and then some.

When I first came to Green Bay, I was a backup linebacker as a rookie. I used to watch the offense and I was amazed at what a machine we had running the ball. I was amazed at Fuzzy and Jerry cutting around the corner, and Ron taking out the linebacker, and Paul and Jimmy running that sweep. Fuzzy wasn't a great big overpowering guy, but he was 99 percent heart. I loved to watch him play.

In Super Bowl I, everybody said Kansas City was close in that first game. The score was 14-10 at halftime, but we had a touchdown called back. The officials said Bob Skoronski was offside, but I looked at that play a hundred times and I still can't see him move. Then, we shut the Chiefs out in the second half. We knew our offense was never going to put us in a bind with bad field position, and Bart Starr wasn't going to throw an interception because that offensive line almost always made the blocks.

We always put our offense above our defense because we felt like offense was the harder job. We felt our job was easier because on defense, we've got 11 guys to stop the running back or the quarterback or the receiver, and they've only got 10 other guys to block you. We always had an advantage, and that's why we felt it was a disservice to ourselves, our families, our coaches, our fans, and our teammates if we didn't make sure the offense's points stood up. We always felt the worse we should ever do in a game is a scoreless tie. It was the way we were trained, and I bought into it.

BOYD DOWLER
WIDE RECEIVER
1959-69

Well, from the beginning, Fuzzy wasn't what you would call an instant success. The Colts cut him. The Bears cut him. He came to Green Bay and nobody knew what he could do. I came in that same year (1959) as a rookie, and the Packers were putting a team together – every part of it – starting with offensive line. They stuck Fuzzy Thurston in there at left guard and Jerry Kramer at right guard and Jim Ringo at center, and Bob Skoronski and Forrest Gregg at the tackles. That line was still together all the way through all of our successful years. Those guys were the starters, and every single one of them was All-Pro or Pro Bowl, and a couple of them made it to the Pro Football Hall of Fame.

The thing that was true about Fuzzy, and very, very obvious from the beginning, was his level of competitiveness. It was there from day one in every single practice, when he played off-season basketball, and I'm sure it was there when he grew up. He had a passion for the game, a passion to do the job, and a passion to do the job the right way. And he did. It wasn't something that happened all of a sudden. It was like he belonged there from day one. He fell into place, and he played the same way all the time.

There wasn't any mystery to it. The only mystery was that he didn't make it with other teams. It didn't bother anybody, though, and it didn't bother him. He had a tremendous amount of talent, but he didn't mention it. He was better than the guys that were playing on those other teams, and he was better than the guys that were here, too.

People make mistakes. Sometimes NFL scouts don't evaluate very well, and sometimes teams don't evaluate their own players very well. He was a whole

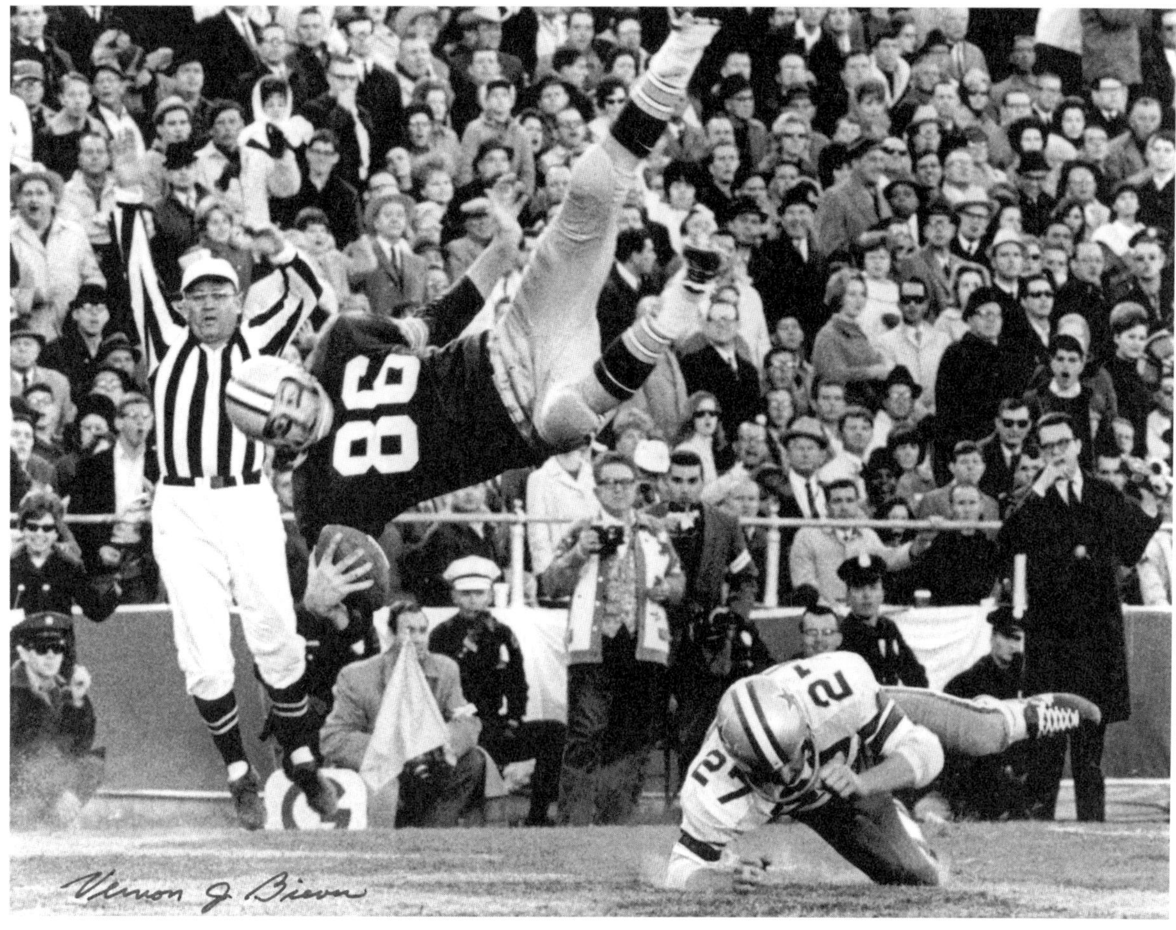

lot better than some guys that were making All-Pro.

Fuzzy's competitiveness shined through from day one. He was going to pass block on Henry Jordan, on Dave Hanner, on all the other guys that lined up in practice. Everything he did, it was like he was playing in a game. When he pulled, and he came around the corner, nobody ever had to remind him to come around full speed. He wasn't looking and searching and tip toeing. He never had to be told twice.

There was nothing cautious about Fred, either. He was total reckless abandon without making mistakes. He knew what to do, and who to do it to. He was a natural.

He and I, and Sue and my wife, Pat, were all close. One of my biggest thrills was being asked to be their daughter Tori's godfather. We were that close. We were roommates for a while, and we just had a natural affection. We bonded. We complimented each other. When it was time to go to dinner after a game, Pat and I would jump in the car and go to Fuzzy's. That's the way it was. That's who we were.

We could always talk. He could tell me how he felt, and I could tell him how I felt. At the end, when he wasn't starting anymore, I remember a time late in his career when Coach Lombardi told him it was time to retire. It was at the 1,000-yard Club Banquet. I'm not sure I was the first one he told, but maybe the second one. I could tell with his voice that his feelings were hurt. He was down. We could share emotions like that, and it wasn't as if I had any magic words to come back with, but I understood how he felt.

That team we put together originally in '59, especially on offense, was our best team. The '61 and '62 teams were the best teams we had. They were better than the Super Bowl teams. We had Jim Ringo, Fuzzy, Max was faster, I was faster, and Jimmy Taylor and Paul Hornung were younger and stronger and quicker. We were just better. And Fuzzy was smack dab in the middle of the whole thing.

I'll never forget Fuzzy in the first Super Bowl. I went down with a shoulder injury and Max came in on the third play. I'm trying to stay out of the way, and Fuzzy came over to me late in the game after we got a lead that was going to hold up. His facemask was all bent up. He was blocking the Chiefs' Buck Buchanon, a future Hall of Fame defensive lineman, and I told Fuzzy his facemask was all bent to hell. He said, "You're damn right it is, and if you were blocking that big son-of-a-bitch all game, your facemask would be all bent up, too." Then he said, "I'm kicking his ass."

We both started to laugh. We could communicate like that. We were friends. We had a chemistry that's hard to explain. We could talk, have a beer together, and take our wives to dinner together. It felt natural because it was. And that's the way it is with relationships. It was always special. That's Fuzzy and that's me. That's how we were. It'll never go away, whether we talk to each other once a week or once a year.

JERRY KRAMER
GUARD
1958-68

Well, I love Fuzzy, first of all, and I admire his attitude and spirit. He's always been to me like a 5-year-old boy on Christmas morning, and he got a bucket of horseshit for Christmas and shouted, "Yippee!" When everyone asked why he was so happy, he'd say, "With all this horseshit, there's got to be a pony around here somewhere." He will find the good and the right in everything.

One of my enduring memories, and there are so many, was when Brett Favre won his first ballgame. It happened on alumni weekend. Favre got the ball with a minute and change, and he had to go 90-some yards, and we scored with just a few seconds left. The extra-point team's on the field waiting for Brett to come back because he was the holder. Well, we make the kick, the Packers win, and the crowd is going nuts.

We were celebrating and hugging and finally we make our way up the tunnel.

Then, I hear the crowd start going nuts again. I turn and walk back down the tunnel, and there was Fuzzy on about the 15 or 20-yard line with that cane up in the air. He was recovering from hip surgery, he's standing there, and the players had left the field. But, Fuzzy was still there and the photographers were around him. As he's thrusting his cane up in the air, he catches my eye, winks at me, and shakes his head for me to come join him. He was having a hell of a time celebrating. He was so exuberant and so believing.

WILLIE WOOD
DEFENSIVE BACK
1960-71

I knew Fuzzy as an outstanding athlete. He had the strength and the poise of a great player. I knew he was going to be there for a long time. He wasn't the biggest player, but he had the strength and the speed and the quickness to overcome it. He was a big fundamentalist. Everything he did was based on fundamentals. That's what kept him in the business so long. He knew what he was doing, all right, and he was one of those guys that brought everybody else together. For that reason, he was very valuable.

He has been the conduit for his past teammates, too. Fuzzy and his wife, Sue, are everybody's brother and sister. He was a great guy. He had a big heart, too. I mean a big heart. What can you say about a guy who has everybody else's feelings at heart?

He was a man. He was a tremendous pass blocker. Everybody knew that. Those guards, they had the speed of a running back, both of them, and I think that getting out in front of those runners like that was Fuzzy's big thing. I think he enjoyed doing that, and consequently, he ended up doing it very well.

Off the field Fuzzy was fun-loving. That was his thing. He made everybody around him happy. Coach Lombardi was tough on him, that was true, but he was tough on all of us. He just knew that Fuzzy was a little mischievous, and that he could take it when he came down on him.

JESSE WHITTENTON
DEFENSIVE BACK
1958-64

Fuzzy was my roommate. He was the best guy with the biggest heart in the world. What else can you say? That guy's got more energy and more desire … that's why nobody would touch him. He worked hard. All he thought about was football. He was a basketball player, not a football player, in college, so he really worked hard at it. Fuzzy was only six feet tall, and that was stretching it, but he was awfully quick. He was a big boy back at that time, and he was naturally strong. Now, he'd be a defensive back.

He's been the glue that has kept our team

together over the years. When we go to Green Bay, it means we're going to Fuzzy's. He's got energy that rubs off on you, and everybody looks forward to seeing him. He was down-to-earth, too, and no goody two-shoes, that's for sure. But, he was a player. Man, he'd come around on that cut-off block, and he was so quick, and he weighed 250 pounds, and he was coming full speed. There was only one thing to do: Get out of the way.

BART STARR
QUARTERBACK
1956-71

Fuzzy was a guy that really loved the game. Gregarious. He was a fun-loving person. He was very committed and, although he was gregarious and appeared to be, at times, somewhat flippant, he was very focused on the game. He wanted to be an outstanding player. That was something you always appreciated because, when you sensed the commitment that they have, it's really nice to know that guy's your teammate. Of course, Jerry Kramer was an outstanding guard, and proportionately received more attention and publicity than Fuzzy, and earned it, but I always thought that Fuzzy was perhaps not given the attention or the credit that he should've been given because he was solid, really solid.

Fuzzy was challenged by Coach Lombardi's challenges, and he would be better the next day. That's why Coach Lombardi took that approach. I would place right at the top, of all Fuzzy's great qualities, was his devotion to the game, his commitment, because it showed. He worked his tail off in practice, he was very studious in meetings, and he was very attentive when coaches were making points on the field. You had confidence in him knowing that he was so studious, and because he was so studious, you knew that when we had to make adjustments preparing for a game – or maybe during a game – that he's going to pick up on it right away and do a great job with it.

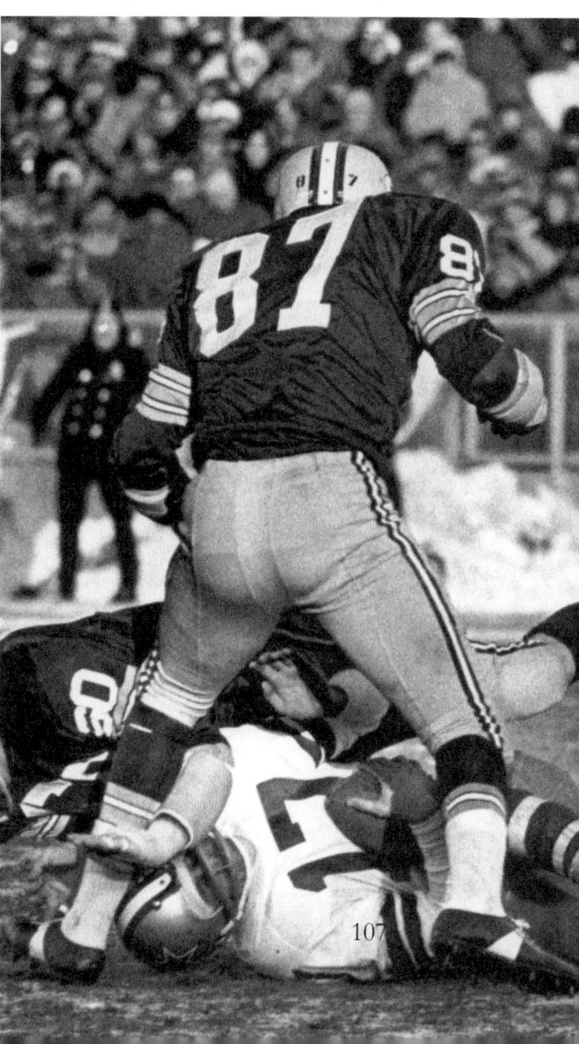

WILLIE DAVIS
DEFENSIVE END
1960-69

You hear the term 'blue-collar' a lot in sports, and football in particular. It's meant to characterize a certain type of individual that was hard-working and spirited. To me, if you were identifying a Green Bay equivalent of 'blue-collar,' that would be several people, but Fuzzy Thurston would clearly be, in my mind, the most logical example.

When they handed out the All-Pros and things, many times Fuzzy wasn't included. But, I always felt that in the game itself, when it came to his assignments and whether it was blocking straight ahead or leading the sweep, he was a guy you could always depend on. He was going to do his absolute best to make sure that his man was taken out of the play, and once that happened, many times he would move on for a second person on the blocking assignment. He will always be one of my favorite individuals as a football player because, in some respect, I thought of myself in the same way.

He was also really outgoing. He was a motivation for our entire team. It seemed like any time we needed to celebrate, or maybe we were down a bit, he would start singing and dancing, and the next thing you knew, the whole team was involved in it.

He has been the glue for our team through the years. When you came back to town, he was the most visible guy. That was part of it, but he would make an effort to make you feel welcomed. He wanted to know how you were doing and if everything was okay. He was the essence of what you would consider a good teammate. He didn't seem to have an enemy around, and that's because he didn't.

Occasionally, people will ask what it was like in Green Bay as far as race and the black-and-white situation. It was guys like Fuzzy that removed any thought of there being some kind of division. He showed as much excitement and absolutely as much respect for any black player as he did for a white player. Fuzzy was great at creating togetherness.

PAUL HORNUNG
HALFBACK
1957-62, 64-66

Well, of course, we were very, very close. He's a great friend, and I learned a long time ago that you've got to get along with your linemen. I would stay at Fuzzy's house in the Fox Valley, and I was close to the kids while they were growing up. Max McGee was my best friend, of course, and then it was Fuzzy and the Kramers (Ron and Jerry). We spent so much time together on the field and off the field. We were at the Left Guard restaurant every Thursday night, Friday night, Sunday night and Monday night.

Fuzzy was a great player. The Baltimore Colts made a huge mistake getting rid of Fuzzy. I never could understand that one. When you looked at Fuzzy, he didn't have the physical attributes that Jerry Kramer had. Kramer was chiseled. Fuzzy got job done nevertheless. He was a very smart player. I've always said we had the smartest football team that ever played the game, and Fuzzy was a big part of that. We played one game against the Chicago Bears that we never called a play in the huddle. We called everything at the line and we didn't make any mistakes. None. Nobody jumped offside. That line was capable of that. We had Fuzzy and Jerry, Jim Ringo and Ken Bowman, and Forrest Gregg probably made fewer mistakes than any of our linemen. If we made mistakes it was more physical than mental.

Fuzzy was great on the sweep. He and Kramer were in tune together. The placement of their feet was unique. When they would cut up the field, Jerry would be a half step ahead of Fuzzy, and by the time they made the turn, Fuzzy would catch up. It had a flow to it. That's the way it should be run. They were the best.

I remember when Coach Lombardi told Fuzzy he was going to retire – not Lombardi, Fuzzy – and it was at the 1,000-yard Club Banquet. If Lombardi hadn't retired him, I think Fuzzy would still be playing. He loved the game that much.

MAX MCGEE
WIDE RECEIVER
1954, 1957-67

Oh, boy, Fuzzy loved to be the left guard on the Green Bay Packers. That's one of the reasons he did such a good job. He came from a small school, Valparaiso, and maybe it meant more to him than somebody else that was from a big school. It mattered a lot to him to be a great guard on a great team.

We were the smartest, if not the biggest team, and Fuzzy represented that. We had college graduates that knew what the hell was going on. If you were going to play for Coach Lombardi, and in particular, if you were going to play offensive line for him, you had to be bright. Things happened in there too fast to have someone that couldn't keep up. You just didn't make mental mistakes with Vince, and if you did, you didn't play.

Off the field, Fuzzy was the fun guy. When we go to Green Bay, to this day, that's the first place we go: Fuzzy's. That name alone attracts attention. Fuzzy. It matches his brain, or that's what I always tell him. We'd start partying a little early in the day on Mondays – our one day off – and we would go to Fuzzy's place. Fuzzy was known for being able to sing and to dance on top of the bar. We couldn't do it because if we fell we might get hurt. Fuzzy could fall off the bar and never get hurt, especially if he fell on his head. Those were the good old days, and Fuzzy was always right there in the heart of it.

Another thing I will say about the Packers and Fuzzy is that there was no prejudice on that team whatsoever. We had great players, black and white, and we enjoyed each other as teammates and men. When we would be out on Mondays drinking and having fun, Willie Davis, Willie Wood, and Herb Adderley, they were right there having fun with us. We weren't making a lot of money, but we were having a lot of fun, and nobody had more fun than Fuzzy.

RON KRAMER
TIGHT END
1957, 1959-64

Fuzzy may have been the best guard in the league. I love Jerry Kramer and Fuzzy both, but Fuzzy consistently had better grades. Jerry was the classic. Fuzzy was the little fuzz ball. Jerry had that great physique, and he was a great promoter of himself, but Fuzzy was a dog-ass guy that would just get in there and play his tail off.

He was a fighter, he had great technique, he was smart, he knew exactly what he was supposed to do, and he didn't have any hang-ups. Jerry was a perfection guy. Fuzzy was the kind of guy that said, "Hey, just play."

We all know the most important thing is not who was better, or more successful, or this or that. The team was the most important thing. I remember when we snuck out in San Francisco, and the next day at practice Coach Lombardi yelled at Fuzzy to get on the line and run wind sprints. He was the only guy that was found out. Well, the rest of us that were with him, we got on the line together. Coach Lombardi loved that. He loved the great feeling that the guys had for each other.

And, of course, Fuzzy and Sue are absolutely wonderful people. I cherish the relationship I have with them and their children. I stayed with them for a time at their house in the Fox Valley. Monday morning the boys would come in and jump on my belly and say, "Let's go fishing. Let's do this. Let's do that." At the time, his kids were my kids, and I loved doing things with them. I think Fuzzy and Sue used me to get rid of the kids so they could have their own time together, and that was fine by me.

DONNY ANDERSON
HALFBACK
1966-71

I have the utmost respect, admiration and love for Fuzzy and Sue. They took me into their home, and they made me feel like part of their family. I felt in some ways like I was their adopted son because I always felt welcome in their home.

Fuzzy took me under his wing right away. I still don't know why but I am grateful that he did. When I signed with the Packers in 1966, I was concerned how the veterans might receive me. I got a lucrative signing bonus, and I thought about all the Packers had accomplished, and that I hadn't really done anything yet. It turns out there wasn't anything to worry about because Fuzzy was there.

He brought me into the group and made

me feel at ease. Fuzzy was a character, too. Whenever there was fun to be had, you can bet Fuzzy was right there in the middle of it. I have so many great stories about Fuzzy's adventures, and they're all true, even if they're unbelievable. He was a great teammate, a great man, and I can't thank him enough for everything he did for a rookie running back a long time ago.

HERB ADDERLEY
DEFENSIVE BACK
1961-69

The first thing I think when I think of Fuzzy Thurston is football, of course, and that he was definitely my best friend during my nine years with the Packers. Our lockers were next to each other, and for those nine years we got to know each other really well. We got to be very good friends.

You have to get along off the field, as well as on the field. We were like a big family, and Fuzzy had a lot to do with bringing everybody together. It was his personality that did it. I always refer to him as a jolly good fellow. He and Willie Davis kept everybody loose or laughing, and as a team, we would get together at someone's home or we'd rent a hotel room downtown and we'd get together, win or lose, and celebrate our friendship and being a team. That had a lot to do with our success and the respect and love for our teammates. It's carried over for years and years, and it still carries over today.

Fuzzy was the guy when it came to singing during training camp. If the rookies were struggling, he would join in with a rendition of "He's got the whole world in his hands." Fuzzy would change it up to say, "He's got the greatest coach in his hands," or "He's got the best pair of guards," or whatever.

I'll never forget the year that Paul Hornung was suspended. Fuzzy started in with, "He's got the gamblin' man in his hands." It got so quiet in the dining hall at St. Norbert College you could've heard a mouse peeing on cotton. There was a table across the room where about six nuns were eating, and all of a sudden they burst out laughing. Then, the whole room laughed, and that included Coach Lombardi. That moment removed any discomfort we might've had about not having Paul with us. We owed it to Fuzzy for being so honest, and to the nuns for making it okay.

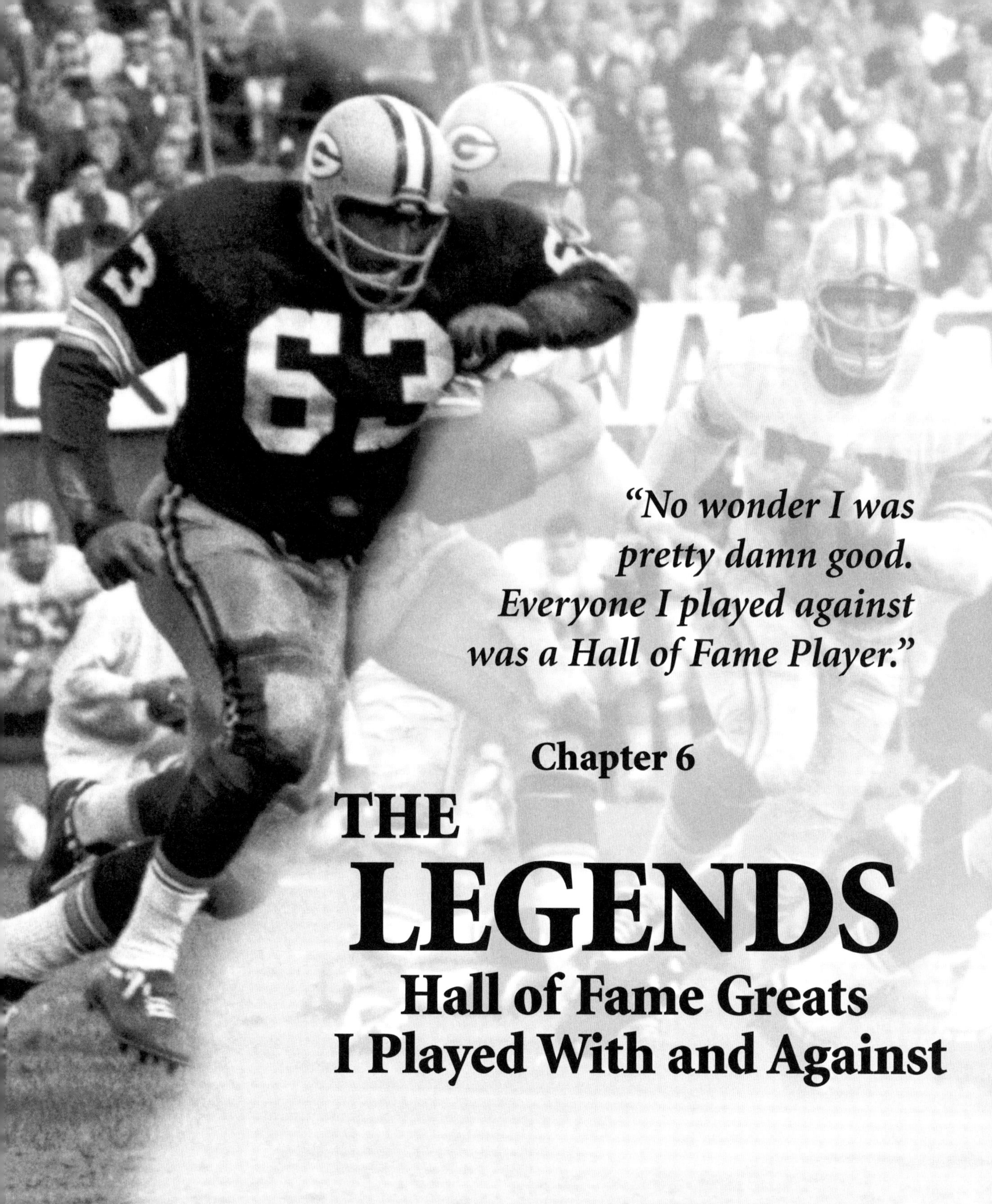

"No wonder I was pretty damn good. Everyone I played against was a Hall of Fame Player."

Chapter 6

THE LEGENDS

Hall of Fame Greats I Played With and Against

Whenever anyone asks me to name a couple of the biggest reasons why I became an All-Pro left guard in the National Football League, I just smile and say, "That's easy. Teammates Henry Jordan and Ron Kostelnik."

I played against some of the NFL's all-time greats, and that includes many players who were eventually inducted into the Pro Football Hall of Fame. However, I owe a tremendous debt of gratitude to the men I practiced against day in and day out in Green Bay. They made me a better football player.

Without a doubt, Henry Jordan was the greatest player I ever lined up against, and I say that with the utmost respect for men such as the Dallas Cowboys' Bob Lilly, the Minnesota Vikings' Alan Page and the Detroit Lions Roger Brown.

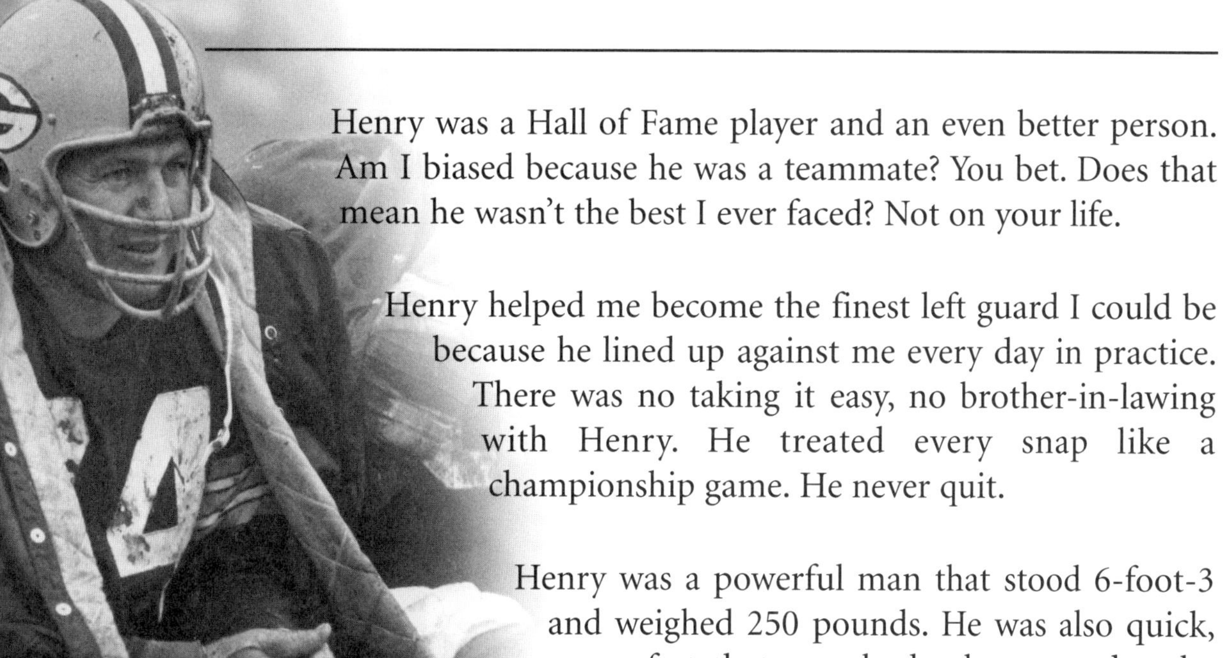

Defensive Tackle Henry Jordan

Henry was a Hall of Fame player and an even better person. Am I biased because he was a teammate? You bet. Does that mean he wasn't the best I ever faced? Not on your life.

Henry helped me become the finest left guard I could be because he lined up against me every day in practice. There was no taking it easy, no brother-in-lawing with Henry. He treated every snap like a championship game. He never quit.

Henry was a powerful man that stood 6-foot-3 and weighed 250 pounds. He was also quick, so fast that everybody else seemed to be moving in slow motion on game day. He became a Hall of Fame player, not because he beat me every day in practice, he became a Hall of Fame player because he beat everybody on game day.

When I lined up on Sunday, I knew it was going to be easier than it was in practice on Thursday and Friday. The only way to get better is in practice, and to have Henry opposite me all those years was a blessing in disguise.

When Henry died at 43, I thought, "Why him and not me?" He was the kindest, gentlest man I ever knew. Henry Jordan's love of football was exceeded only by the love he had for his family. It wasn't fair that he died so young, and to this day, I can honestly say that I'm still not over it.

When we were walking out of the church after Henry's funeral it was raining and there was a big thunderclap. Paul (Hornung) turned to my wife, Sue, and said, "The old man (Coach Vince Lombardi) isn't happy."

I was so very proud when Henry got inducted into the Pro Football Hall of Fame in Canton Ohio.

Ron Kostelnik wasn't as quick as Henry, but he was bigger and stronger. He stood an immovable 6-foot-2 and weighed 270 pounds, and he loved to bull rush. There was no dancing around when you lined up against Ron. He just bull rushed you and knocked the piss out of you. It was like that play after play after play. By the time he got through with you in practice, you couldn't wait for the game because it wouldn't hurt as much.

Ron and I became good friends, despite the daily beatings, because neither one of us could afford to be fined for being overweight. We were diet buddies. Coach Lombardi would fine us $50 for every pound that we were overweight, and in those days that was a lot of money.

So Ron and I wouldn't eat for two days. Then we would weigh in, sigh with relief, and immediately sneak into the back room to start wolfing down sandwiches, one after another, that we placed there exactly for that purpose.

Sometimes, after making weight while we were pigging out, we'd just look at each other and start laughing. Two grown men playing for the World Champion Green Bay Packers, and here we were sneaking around like a couple of school kids. Man, those were great times.

Before Henry Jordan and Ron Kostelnik in Green Bay, there was Art Donovan, Big Daddy Lipscombe and Gino Marchetti in Baltimore. Imagine that. Here I was a kid from little old Valparaiso, and I had an opportunity to practice against five of the greatest defensive linemen that ever wore an NFL uniform.

Tackle Ron Ko

The Colts were World Champions and their defensive line was one of the all-time greatest in NFL history.

Art Donovan had more heart and love for the game than anyone else. He was a bitch to play against, and I love him to this day because he was so good and so special. He didn't have to be nice to me, or work with me, but he did it anyway.

Art wanted the team to be as good as it could be. He knew that if he worked with me, it would make the team that much better. Very rarely did you see veterans do that, but he was one-of-a-kind.

Make that two-of-a-kind because Gino Marchetti was cut from the same cloth. I didn't have to line up against Gino, but he still took time to give me tips and advice on how to handle a pass rusher off the edge. He would say, "You never know when something might come up, and all of a sudden you're out there and left to do it, so let's work on it a little bit."

Then there was Big Daddy, and let me tell you, the nickname fit. When Big Daddy stood up you couldn't see anybody for three miles. I later learned another reason they called him Big Daddy, but that is a story for another day, as this is a family book. He was so tough, and he had a great spin move, but he was really kind, too. He also took time to help me with my game.

I liked everybody, and everybody liked me, so they didn't mind helping me. If somebody likes you on a football team, they'll help you. If they don't like you, they won't. Art, Gino and Big Daddy thought I was a good person, and they enjoyed me, so they worked with me. They showed me all the moves of a defensive lineman and it made me a better player.

The thing with Art and Big Daddy, and then later with Henry and Ron, was that they both were so different. They gave you different looks so you were prepared for anything and everything. Art and Ron were so strong, Big Daddy and Henry were so quick and light on their feet, and all four of them had great hands.

No wonder I was a pretty damn good player. Everybody I played against in practice was a Hall of Fame player. Every time you went out to the practice field – every time you ran a play – you knew you were going against the very best.

That's how I got started. In Baltimore against those great Colts linemen, and it carried over to Green Bay. I got a lot of confidence because I knew I could play against the best. If I could block them, I figured I could block anybody.

I was short for a guard, about 6-foot-1, and I weighed 245 pounds, but my lack of height actually gave me an advantage. I could get leverage on just about everyone I played against. I could get underneath them and they weren't going anywhere.

The guys that gave me trouble were the really quick guys like Henry. If you made the first move against Henry you were a dead duck. He was so quick he could counteract anything you threw at him. So I learned that I had to be patient and wait him out.

Now, in the NFL, if you throw a successful block on 65 to 70 percent of the plays, you're considered one of the very best. You can't block anyone all the time, but because I had such great opponents and teammates to learn from, nothing really surprised me. I knew what I could do, and I did it.

The offensive line coaches that I had helped me with technique, but more important they were there to make sure I knew what the defensive tackle was going to do.

7 Packers Coaching Staff:
L to R: Bob Shnelker-Receivers, Ray Wietecha - Offensive Line, Dave aner-Defensive Line, Phil Bengston-Defense. Bottom L to R: Jerry Burns-ensive Backfield, Head Coach Vince Lombardi, Tom McCormick-ensive Backfield.

When I came to Green Bay, Coach Lombardi brought in Bill Austin to coach the offensive line from 1959 to 1964. Coach Austin went on to become the Head Coach in Pittsburgh and then in Washington. Ray Wietecha came in after Bill left for the Steelers' job. He was with me from 1965 to 1968.

Bill and Ray were very good at watching film and figuring out what my opponent was going to attempt to do. By the time I had been in Green Bay a few years, the technique wasn't an issue; it was trying to outguess the opponent. After the first series or two of a game, you pretty much knew what you were facing. As an offensive lineman, you have to decide if you're going to hold back, like you might against Henry, or if you're going to be aggressive and attack and take the fight to the other man.

There is a lot of psychology that goes with playing on the offensive line. That's why you don't see too many dummies lined up there. It's too hard, and everything happens too fast for someone to succeed who isn't a student of the game.

Jerry Kramer and Fuzzy Thurston lead the legendary Packers sw

It's important for fans to know that, in our era, the defensive tackles almost always lined up in the same spot. They were either a right tackle or a left tackle, which meant I almost always lined up against the same tackle, and Jerry Kramer did, too. That meant Kramer didn't have to block Alan Page or Bob Lilly, but he did have to block the Los Angeles Rams' Merlin Olsen and the Detroit Lions' Alex Karras. We both had our hands full, but we also got the job done.

To this day, the Packers are the only team that had a Hall of Fame backfield – Paul Hornung and Jim Taylor – playing together at the same time. Now, I would like someone to explain this to me: How can a team have the only pair of Hall of Fame backs in NFL history, but still not have either guard in the Hall of Fame? It makes no sense.

We were a team, not individuals. If that meant we wouldn't be voted into the Hall of Fame – and by we, I mean Jerry Kramer and me – I can live with that.

I loved playing guard opposite Jerry, and I loved lining up next to Bob Skoronski all those years. Bob was a terrific left tackle, and we were just so comfortable together, it was second nature. The funny thing is, it was like that from day one. I just knew that Bob was never, ever going to make a mistake. I don't think he jumped offside once in all the years we played together. I doubt if he was ever called for a holding penalty, either, because we ran so much and passed so little.

This is how well Bob and I knew each other and worked together: Not only did we know our own man, we knew the other guy's man, too. For instance, whenever we were going to play the Chicago Bears, Bob would always say, "Whatever you do don't get Doug Atkins mad. Don't cut him. Don't block him in the back. Don't rile him up."

Bob's reasoning was simple. When Atkins, who was a 6-foot-8, 275-pound monster, would get angry there was no stopping him. Bob would say, "Don't piss him off because there's nobody in the world that can block him when he's pissed."

Atkins, who was also a Hall of Fame player, used to tease me during games. He would come up to the line and start saying, "Poor old Fuzzy. Nobody wanted Fuzzy. Now he's stuck in Green Bay with his five World Championship rings. Poor old Fuzzy."

Atkins liked me, I think, which was a good thing. He was as tough a player as there was, and he made a lot better friend than enemy. That's why it was so important for us to play together.

When you play with a guy all those years, if there was any way we could help each other we would. Fortunately, we had the ability to take care of ourselves. That's the thing with five, six, seven players that are good. You

Fuzzy Thurston and Bob Skoro

take care of your job and you don't have a weakness. We played with basically the same offensive guards and tackles the entire time I played in Green Bay. We developed into a consistent and cohesive unit. With free agency, that just doesn't happen in the NFL anymore. I believe it was the key to our success. We made defenses worry about the run, so when we passed it was a lot easier. We had them on their heels before the ball was snapped.

It was enjoyable to play next to such a consummate pro as Bob Skoronski. It made going to work that much more fun, and it made winning games that much easier. I relied on Bob, and Bob relied on me, because there was nothing easy about the men we went against. It seemed every week we went up against a Hall of Fame player.

The Minnesota Vikings' Alan Page was a rangy 6-foot-4 with long arms, great balance and the quickest first move you could imagine. He played at 225 pounds, which is small by today's standards, but back then he was big enough, and because of his long arms, you really couldn't get into him.

Page was as durable as they come. He played in 218 straight games and four Super Bowls. He was all over the field. You felt like you were chasing him all day long. Straight up the field, sideways, backwards, he was quick.

Page was smart, too. He ended up becoming a judge, and I'm not surprised because he was a brilliant man. He would try to beat you, not beat you up. He could outsmart the best of them with his quickness and his knowledge. He also had terrific hands to go with those long arms, and it felt like they were all over your body.

The Dallas Cowboys' Bob Lilly was a rare combination of power and speed. He was as fast as Page, or damn near, and as strong as the Detroit Lions' Roger Brown. He stood 6-foot-5 and weighed a well-chiseled 260 pounds. Lilly had it all. You had to work your butt off against him just to keep from being embarrassed. He was one of the top four or five defensive tackles that ever played the game, and that includes everybody that came before or since.

Bob Lilly, Defensive Tackle, Dallas Cowboys

The Cowboys let Lilly two-gap holes, which is to say, they let him go either direction against the offensive guard. And they would cover the hole he vacated with a middle linebacker to protect him. He was quick enough to go with a pulling guard and chase the play down from the backside. He would just beat the running back to the hole, or he would go outside and try to get a pass rush.

Dallas let him have a lot of freedom to shoot gaps, and he did a lot of spin moves. He was very, very disruptive. He was always aggressive, and he was as good as anybody I ever played against. I always thought that if Lilly made a play, we goofed up, because we felt like we should be able to block anybody.

When it came to Dick Butkus, the great Chicago Bears' middle linebacker, nobody had a greater will to win. Quite literally, the man played like a caged animal.

Good ol' Butkus. You talk about a football player that loved the game, you talk about a guy that would shake hands, you talk about a guy that would then go out and kick your butt, you're talking about Butkus.

In my opinion, the two best middle linebackers that ever played the game were Butkus and Ray Nitschke... or Nitschke and Butkus. Who was better? Nobody cared. They both had their strengths and their weaknesses, but I can't tell you what their weaknesses were.

Butkus could do everything. He could blitz, nobody tackled better, he could cover backs out of the backfield, he had great feet for a big guy, he was 6-foot-3 and he weighed 245 pounds. He didn't look fast, though. In fact, he looked

Ray Nitschke

clumsy at times. But, he got there. He always got there.

Dick Butkus - Middle Linebacker, Chicago Bears

I guess if I had to say he had a weakness, it was that he tried to make every play. Sometimes he was too aggressive and he would overshoot and make a mistake. Most of the time that happened in pass protection when he would get excited, take a step, and then realize he had to cover the tight end.

Nitschke and Butkus never played head-to-head, obviously, but when the Packers and the Bears played, everybody in the stadium knew the battle was on. Nitschke and Butkus knew how good the other one was and they wanted to be better. Ray wanted to be better than Butkus, and the other way around. It inspired them to have great games. You can take that to the bank.

The Bears had another good linebacker, a great linebacker, a Hall of Fame linebacker, in the 1960s before Butkus. That was Bill George.

George wasn't very big, maybe 6-foot-2 and 230 pounds, and he wasn't overpowering, but he was very, very smart. He was a finesse middle linebacker and probably the smartest linebacker in the whole bunch. He knew everything about everybody, and he covered running backs out of the backfield like a cornerback.

#70 Sam Huff - Linebacker New York Giants

He was also very kind to me during my short time with the Bears. He was another player who took the time to help a younger player if he liked him and the player sincerely wanted to be better, because Bill George knew it helped the team.

The Detroit Lions' Joe Schmidt and the New York Giants' Sam Huff were also excellent linebackers and men I played against fairly regularly. Schmidt was good because he was so very quick and excellent in the passing game.

Huff was a different type of player. He wanted to make all the plays, and therefore he goofed up at times. If he had a weakness, that was it. He took himself out of position too many times. We would pull the guards and come right back to that spot and he would be gone already.

Huff played in New York, so he got a lot of publicity. I'm sure he was one of the best that played at that time, but he was no Butkus, no Nitschke, and no Bill George. He was a very good player, but he wasn't in that class.

The Kansas City Chiefs' Buck Buchanan was huge – he stood 6-foot-7 and weighed 274 pounds – and I'll never forget what the writers were writing before Super Bowl I. They all wanted to know, "Who was going to block Buck Buchanan?"

Buck was the biggest, fastest, quickest and meanest player I had ever read about. How in the world could a short 265 pound guard block him? Well, I blocked him all day and he never touched the quarterback and we scored right over him. I showed Buck Buchanan who Fuzzy Thurston was. He was supposed to be the best I ever faced. He wasn't. He was good. He was very good, but he wasn't the best that I ever played against.

One of the best I did play against was Roger Brown of the Detroit Lions. He was No. 1 in my book. He didn't make it into the Pro Football Hall of Fame, and for the life of me, I don't know why. He was so big and strong (he was 6-foot-2 and he weighed 320 pounds) that he would just overpower the guard he played against. I played at about 265 pounds, which was my highest weight, and he played at a strong 320, and he was quick to boot. If he wasn't as quick as I was, there were days when it sure seemed like it.

Roger Brown came at you every play, and he'd knock the hell out of you. It was very tough on the body, and it wore you out. I tried to play against him on a Thanksgiving Day at Detroit in 1962 with a separated right shoulder. We were 10-0 going into the Detroit game. As a matter of fact, my wife Sue and I named our baby daughter Victoria, short for victory, following her birth on November 1st of that year.

I had injured that shoulder against the Baltimore Colts on the Sunday before the Lions game, and we had to play that Thursday. Four days just wasn't enough rest, and Roger Brown was too much. He beat me four or

#76 Roger Brown, Detroit Lions. The 1962 Thanksgiving Day game was Green Bay's only loss of the season

five times. He got to Bart (Starr) at least that many times. It was the worst game I ever played in the NFL. After the game, I retreated to the locker room. I did not speak to any of my teammates and they did not speak to me. I was disappointed in myself and I was also in terrible pain, both physically and emotionally. There were reasons I played poorly, but it didn't make me feel any better.

Coach Lombardi knew that I had a shoulder problem, but it didn't matter. He had to be Coach Lombardi, and if you got beat, he would tell the world about it. And by the world, I don't mean the press. I mean your teammates.

It was terrible watching the film from that game. We lost 26-17 and you would have thought the world was collapsing.

The week leading up to the Detroit game was one of the worst of my life. I separated my shoulder against the Colts on Sunday. On Monday, I received word that my mother had passed away. My mother was the most important person in the world to me, and the news had a profound negative effect. I locked myself in the bedroom and would not speak to anyone, not even my wife, Sue. At that moment, not even she could help me. That is the first and last time I can ever recall wanting to be left completely alone. It was so painful. My mother was too young to die and it was a big loss. With a heavy heart and a feeling of overwhelming sadness, I somehow had to prepare to attend practice for the Thanksgiving game and then to say good-bye to my mother. Her funeral was held the day after the Thanksgiving game with the Lions.

I knew I had to go on, and my mother had always taught me that things were not always as bad as you think they are. By Tuesday, I had managed to get myself out of that locked bedroom and give it my best effort. Predictably, I just couldn't compete to the best of my abilities. After the loss to Detroit, because they beat us so bad, a lot of stories were written. One said that "Fuzzy Thurston – who was blocking Roger Brown, and not very often – turned around and said, 'Look out, Bart. Here he comes again.'"

That never happened, but I used it on the banquet circuit and I never got a bigger laugh. When you tell a story about yourself, and it's self-deprecating, it's the best thing you can do. Why pretend he didn't beat you?

I do have to say that Bart was amazing because he never complained, not once, even when he was getting the hell beat out of him (which wasn't very often). Bart never criticized me. He never criticized Jerry or Forrest or any of us. If he got sacked, we never heard about it. He was the greatest. He took all of the punishment and he never blamed anybody. Bart knew this wasn't an easy job, and he knew nobody was going to do it one hundred percent all the time. Now, he got upset, naturally, but he knew it was a team. He wouldn't say, "Fuzzy, get that damn block." He would say, "Hey, guys. Let's get that guy blocked."

It's different with today's players. You hear some quarterbacks blaming their offensive line in the press conferences and to anyone else who will listen. If Bart had tried something like that back when we played, he would've gotten a serious poke in the jaw. But, Bart wouldn't do it because Bart was a team player. I didn't want to disappoint Bart or my teammates. If I made a mistake, I played even harder. The next Detroit game was a great example. I wasn't going to let Roger Brown anywhere near Bart.

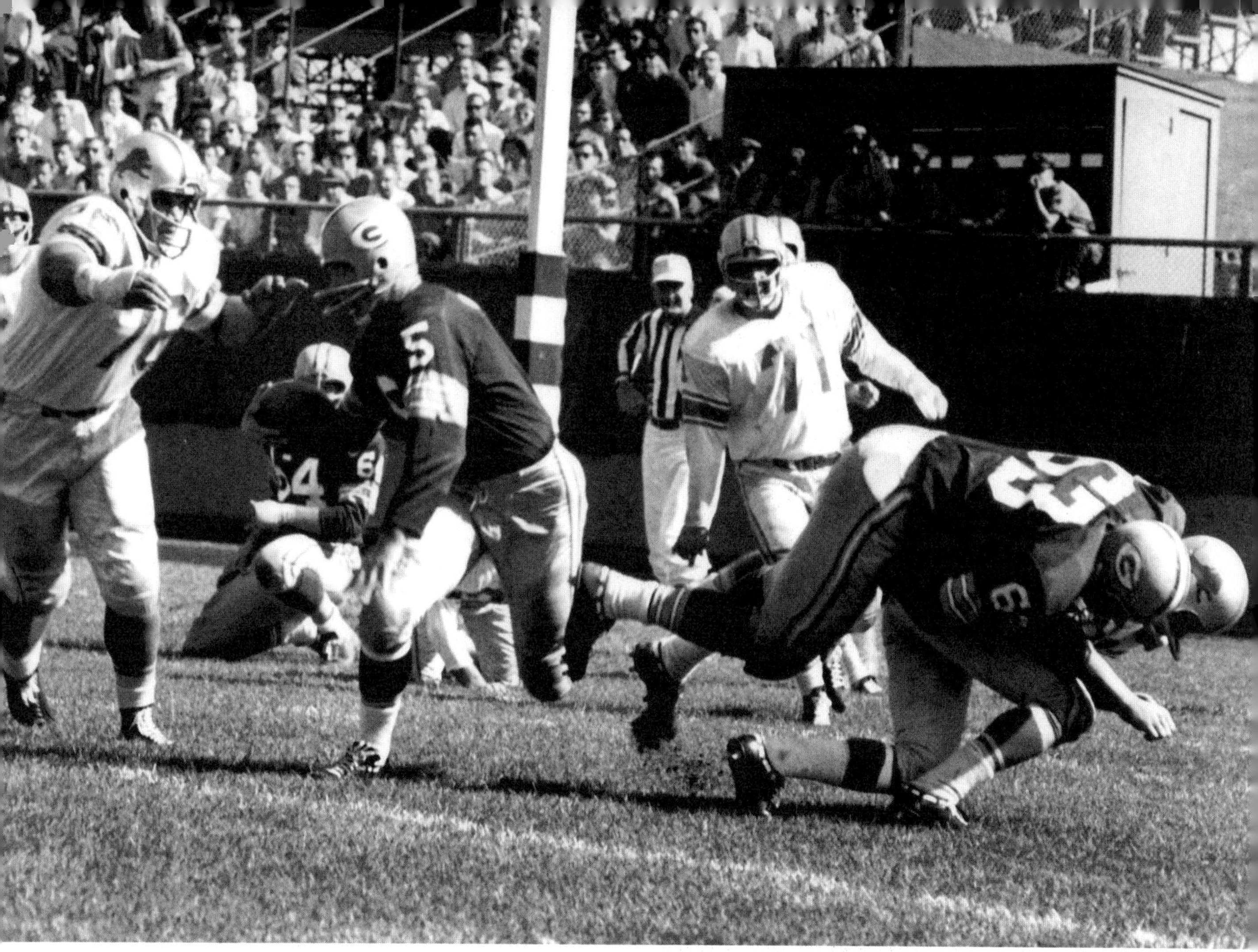

The tables turn. The Packers win the 1963 Milwaukee game vs Detroit. L to R, Bart Starr (15), Roger Brown (76), Jerry Kramer (64), Paul Hornung (5) and Fuzzy Thurston (63).

Early next season, we beat Detroit 31-10 in Milwaukee, and I'm not sure if Roger Brown got close enough to Bart to know what jersey number he was wearing. I got the game ball because I blocked Roger Brown 100 percent. He didn't beat me once.

Why the change from one year to the next? First, I was healthy, I was in great shape, and I knew we were going to play the Lions and Brown in the second game. I started getting ready for that rematch in July. From that day on, I always did a great job against him. He beat me once in a while, but it was never the problem that it was on that Thanksgiving Day in 1962.

After the game against Detroit in 1963, Coach Lombardi presented the game ball to me and said, "Gentlemen, you just saw one of the greatest efforts by an offensive guard in the history of the game. Congratulations, Fuzzy." It was rare for anyone to receive that kind of recognition and admiration from Coach Lombardi. It was one of the proudest moments in my career, and to this day that ball is one of my most prized possessions.

PRO FOOTBALL HALL OF FAME PLAYERS I PLAYED WITH AND AGAINST

Listed below are some of the Pro Football Hall of Fame players that Fuzzy Thurston went head-to-head against in practice and games. It includes defensive tackles and middle linebackers

(Source: NFL Record & Fact Book).

CHUCK BEDNARIK

MIDDLE LINEBACKER, PHILADELPHIA EAGLES • 6-3, 230

Bednarik played for the Eagles from 1949-62. He is regarded as one of the most rugged linebackers in NFL history. Packers' fans recall Bednarik wrestling fullback Jim Taylor to the ground at the 8-yard line, and then refusing to let him up as time expired in Philadelphia's 17-13 victory in the 1960 NFL Championship game at Philadelphia's Franklin Field. Bednarik, an eight-time Pro Bowl linebacker, missed three games during 14 NFL seasons.

BUCK BUCHANAN

DEFENSIVE TACKLE, KANSAS CITY CHIEFS • 6-7, 274

Buchanan played for the Chiefs from 1963-75. He led the Chiefs' defensive efforts in Super Bowl I, IV. He did not miss a game in 13 years. Buchanan and Thurston squared off in Super Bowl I.

DICK BUTKUS

MIDDLE LINEBACKER, CHICAGO BEARS • 6-3, 245

Butkus played for the Bears from 1965-73. He was an All-NFL player six years, and he played in eight consecutive Pro Bowls. He recovered an NFL-record 25 fumbles. Butkus and Thurston tangled twice each season from 1965-68.

ART DONOVAN

DEFENSIVE TACKLE, BALTIMORE COLTS • 6-3, 265

Donovan played for the Colts from 1953-61. He was a five-time Pro Bow player that was vital in Baltimore's climb to powerhouse status in the 1950s. Donovan and Thurston were teammates in 1958, and later faced each other from 1959-61.

BILL GEORGE

MIDDLE LINEBACKER, CHICAGO BEARS • 6-2, 230

George played for the Bears from 1952-65. He was All-NFL for eight years and he played in eight consecutive Pro Bowls. He had 14 years of NFL service, the longest of any Bears player. George and Thurston battled twice each season from 1959-65.

SAM HUFF

MIDDLE LINEBACKER, NEW YORK GIANTS • 6-1, 230

Huff played for the Giants from 1964-67. He had 30 interceptions and played in six NFL title games and five Pro Bowls. Huff and Thurston met numerous times in the mid-1960s.

HENRY JORDAN

DEFENSIVE TACKLE, GREEN BAY PACKERS • 6-3, 240

Jordan played for the Packers from 1959-69. He was a fixture at defensive tackle during the Packers' dynasty. He played in four Pro Bowls, seven NFL title games and Super Bowl I and Super Bowl II. Jordan and Thurston were best friends off the field and fierce competitors during practice.

BOB LILLY

DEFENSIVE TACKLE, DALLAS COWBOYS • 6-5, 260

Lilly played for the Cowboys from 1961-74. He played in 11 Pro Bowls and 196 consecutive games. Lilly and Thurston went helmet-to-helmet numerous times during the 1960s, including the now-famous Ice Bowl.

GINO MARCHETTI

DEFENSIVE END, BALTIMORE COLTS • 6-4, 245

Marchetti played for the Colts from 1953-64, 66. He was named the NFL's top defensive end of the league's first 50 years. He went to 10 consecutive Pro Bowls and was All-NFL seven times. Marchetti and Thurston never faced each other in games, but when they were Colts teammates in 1958, Marchetti went out of his way to work with Thurston on his pass-blocking technique.

RAY NITSCHKE

MIDDLE LINEBACKER, GREEN BAY PACKERS • 6-3, 235

Nitschke played for the Packers from 1958-72. He was MVP of the 1962 title game and named the NFL's all-time linebacker in 1969. Nitschke and Thurston were friends and teammates, and Thurston credits Nitschke with helping his own development by going full speed in practice.

ALAN PAGE

DEFENSIVE TACKLE, MINNESOTA VIKINGS • 6-4, 225

Page played for the Vikings from 1967-78. He was a dominating defensive tackle that played in 218 consecutive games and four Super Bowls. He was the NFL's MVP in 1971. Page and Thurston squared off twice each season in 1967 and 1968.

JOE SCHMIDT

MIDDLE LINEBACKER, DETROIT LIONS • 6-0, 222

Schmidt played for the Lions from 1953-65. He had 24 interceptions and was Detroit's team captain for nine years. Schmidt and Thurston did battle from 1959-65.

Upper left hand corner: Fuzzy, his mother and brothers
Below: Receiving an award from the Army - Fuzzy and his mother - Upper right: Fuzzy played for the Packers' traveling basketball team - Below: Fuzzy and his brothers.

Top of page: Paul Hornung, Fuzzy, Sue and friends at a 1000-Yard Club Banquet -
- Fuzzy with a young fan - Boyd Dowler and his wife

left: Fuzzy, the Thurston kids and teammates - Upper right: Fuzzy and Jerry Kramer
ng a high fashion look in fur for a magazine advertisement - Bottom left: Fuzzy and
tarr look on as Jerry Kramer and Jimmy Taylor arm wrestle
n Right: Fuzzy signs autographs for three beauty queens

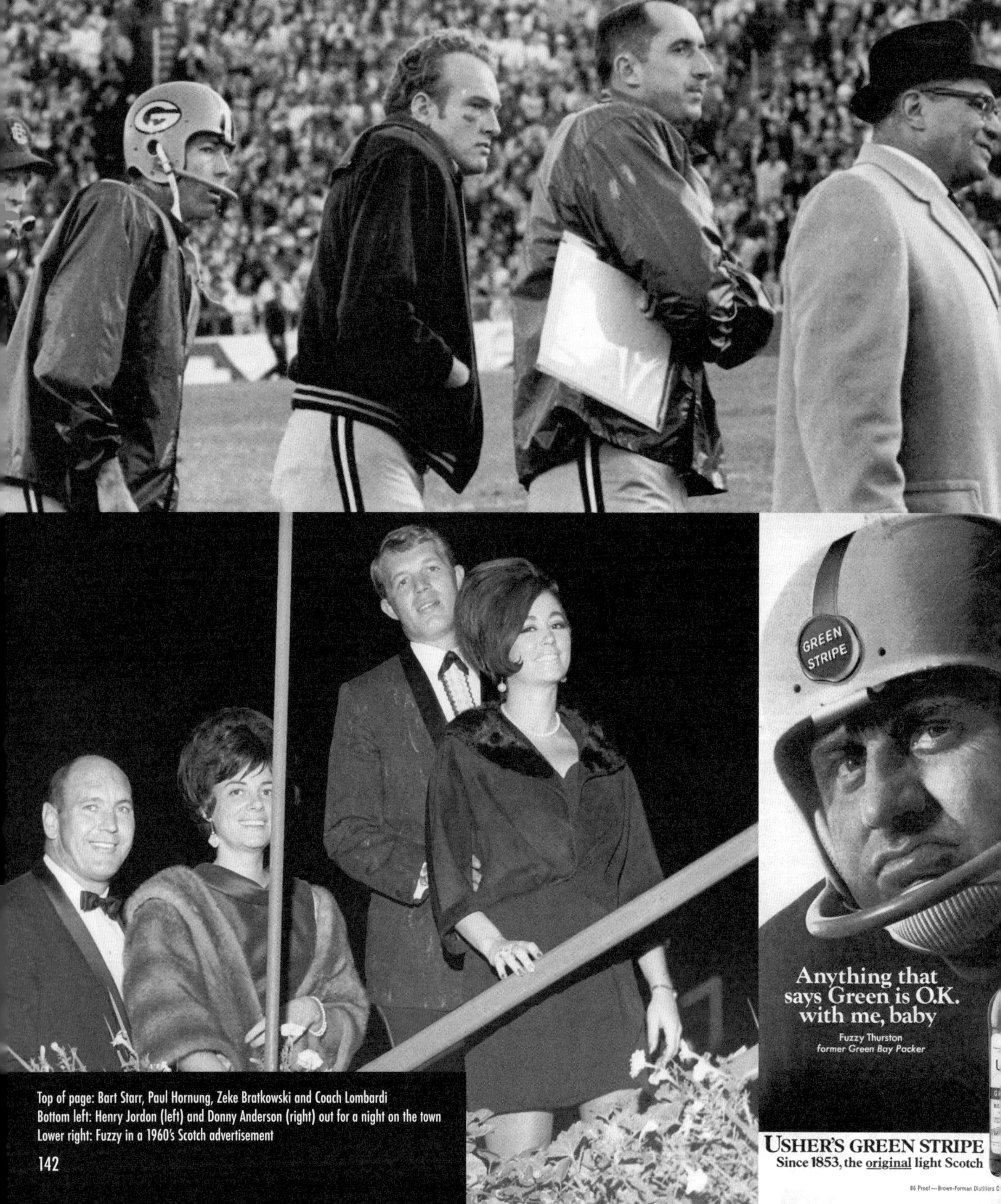

Top of page: Bart Starr, Paul Hornung, Zeke Bratkowski and Coach Lombardi
Bottom left: Henry Jordon (left) and Donny Anderson (right) out for a night on the town
Lower right: Fuzzy in a 1960's Scotch advertisement

The final farewell to the beloved coach

Fuzzy & Friends: Upper left: Max McGee, Paul Hornung
Below (clockwise from left): Boyd Dowler - Vince Lombardi Jr. - Herb Adderley
Right (from top): Jerry Kramer, Paul Hornung - Willie Davis - Jerry Kramer - Paul Hornung

Fuzzy and his famous friends - Upper left: President Gerald Ford with Paul Hornung and Fuzzy - Below: Howard Cosell, Fuzzy & Sue Thurston, and Jack Klugman - Jerry Kramer, Reggie White - Upper Right: Don Meredith when he was a guest on Fuzzy's TV show - Below: Lee Trevino Bottom right: Meatloaf, who borrows Fuzzy's name when traveling incognito

Please accept this gift
as an expression of our
sincere gratitude for all
you have done for the
Green Bay Packers.
Vince Lombardi

Fuzzy and Family: Upper right: Note from Coach Lombardi to Sue Thurston enclosed with his gift of a mink stole - Bottom left: Griff Thurston, Sue, Fuzzy and grandchildren, Olivia and Freddy - Above: Paul Hornung and wife with Tori Thurston - Bottom Right: Fuzzy and his grandson Joey

Good to see you again Fuzzy

BILL CALLS WAITER TO CLEAR GLASSES AS VINCE ARRIVES!!

Jane sneaks a picture of Dr. Casey

MATTEOS REST. L.A.

Ben Casey shakes hands with two REAL celebrities!!!

The girls take a walk on Wilshire Blvd.

Two hours before "The Game" in front of the Sheraton-West

"THE GIRLS"

Willie does the honors for the Family Portrait

SUPER BOWL 1967

Kansas City shows early confidence

Jim + Jane at the Sheraton-West

Off to the game

Bill spots the "foot long" hot dog

Tony Canadeo + Ray Scott going into "The Office" for a pleasant day's work

Early arrivals

Some anxious moments early in the game

The Grambling Band is really colorful!

Vince's friend leaves the dressing room minus his rifle

GUESS WHO WON??

Not bad pay for an afternoon's work Henry!!

Frank Gifford solves the transportation problem after the game

Herb and Susan at Villa Nova

Paul tells Fuzzy that the wedding is Wed. + the Bishop wasn't a bad guy at all to do business with!

Susan, don't look so enthused!

Phil Crosby is a Packer fan all the way

Chivalry is not dead

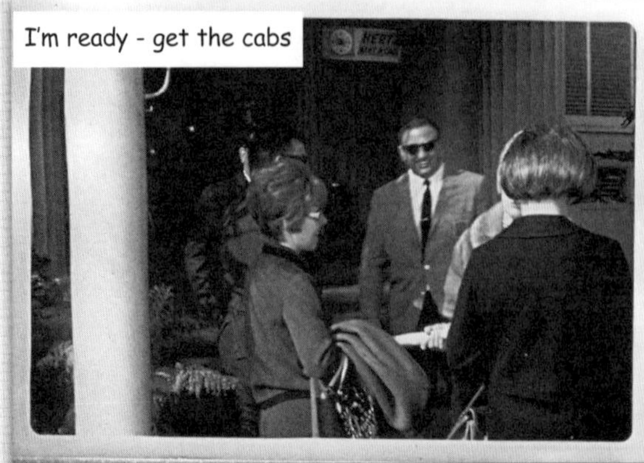
I'm ready - get the cabs

Herb just told Meredith that this table was for winners only

WE'LL BE BACK FOR PAUL'S WEDDING
VEGAS, HERE WE COME!

ON TO THE TABLES!!

"What do I do with my life, whatever life I may have left?

What's going to happen to my wife and kids?"

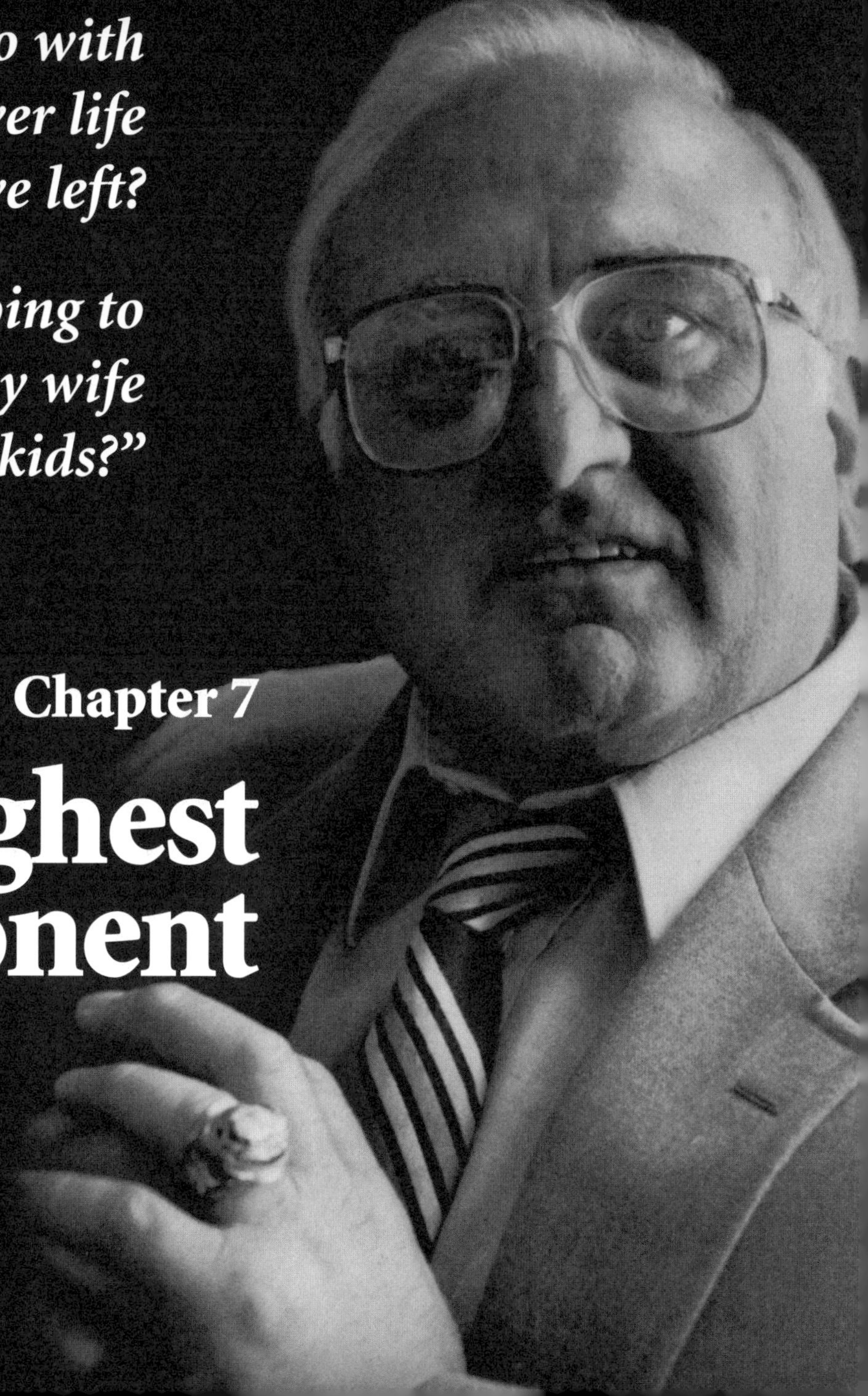

Chapter 7

My Toughest Opponent

I was scared when I started my first NFL game. What if I broke my ankle on the first play? What if I got injured and never had a chance to prove to anyone that I belonged? What if?

Looking back, I feel foolish, perhaps even embarrassed. I had no idea what fear was until the day my doctor told me I had cancer. That was in 1980.

The previous fall, my wife, Sue, repeatedly told me I sounded different, like I had a frog in my throat. She urged me on numerous occasions to go see a doctor. I was feeling fine, so I ignored the warning signs. Finally, I came to terms with the fact that something was wrong.

I scheduled an appointment with Dr. Tim Donovan, an ear, nose and throat specialist in Madison. After one look at my throat, and not much deliberation, I was immediately scheduled for a biopsy. It would be a week before the procedure could be done. I was nervous. So many negative thoughts were racing in my mind. I thought about the "C" word. What if it was cancer? I felt fine, so I worked on convincing myself that it was nothing. That week, Sue and I didn't talk very much about the biopsy. We thought the less we talked about it, the less real the situation would seem. A week later, I had the biopsy.

Sue was in the waiting room. Shortly after the procedure, the doctor appeared. The news was bad; I had cancer. Sue later told me that upon hearing the news she experienced overwhelming panic and fear. The doctor told Sue that she could see me, but not to say a word about the cancer. He wanted to be there to tell me and explain the treatment options. When Sue walked in I could immediately tell that something was terribly wrong. I didn't have to hear the news to know it was bad. I could see it on her face. Afterwards, Dr. Donovan confirmed the worst. He told me I had cancer of the vocal chords. I was stunned. I had a thousand questions, but I all I could do was just sit there without saying a word. I thought to myself, "Am I going to die?"

I felt numb, but somehow I managed to get on my feet and walk outside. Then I started to cry. Where do I go from here? What do I do with my life, whatever life I may have left? What's going to happen to my wife and kids? Do I pray? Do I go to Mass? I began thinking about the little things that used to worry me and how trivial they seemed at that time. I knew I was in trouble. I had cancer of the vocal chords. In order to halt the cancer and save my life, the doctors recommended surgery to remove one of my vocal chords, followed by a series of radiation treatments. The doctors couldn't guarantee that I would be able to talk after surgery, let alone survive.

I was upset with myself for not listening to Sue's advice. She told me to see a doctor because something was not right. Why was I so stubborn? I thought my voice sounded just fine. I thought it was no big deal. I thought that right up until the moment the doctor and Sue gave me the bad news.

Finally, after I stopped crying outside the doctor's office, I did what I always did in a stressful situation. I reached into my pocket, pulled out my smokes, and just stared at them. I didn't feel like the Marlboro Man right then, so I grabbed the pack of cigarettes, crushed it in my right hand and threw it away. I haven't smoked since.

I looked at the Marlboros in the trash, wondered if smoking had caused the cancer, and decided it didn't matter. I had bigger problems now.

Leading up to the surgery, Sue and I tried to go about our daily routine and avoid the topic as much as possible. We were both very scared. After the surgery, I could talk a little, but my voice was gravely. I sounded like Ray Nitschke with a bad cold. My throat hurt like hell, even a week after the surgery. The surgery was followed by a series of radiation treatments. The combination of the two was the best shot at stopping the cancer. I drove back and forth to Madison for the treatments. Many times, Sue had to stay behind and run the business. As if fighting the cancer wasn't enough, my business was also in trouble. We were faced with enormous financial challenges, but stopping the cancer and getting well was really all that mattered.

The treatment lasted about 6 months. During that time, I started exercising. I had been retired from football for 12 years and hadn't taken really good care of myself. Truthfully, I was totally out of shape. I began walking and exercising. I figured that no matter how bad I felt, a good workout would make me feel better. It was good therapy for my mind and body.

I was starting to feel healthy again. The treatments were over, life was getting back to normal, and by all accounts the cancer was in remission. I felt like I was out of the woods and had dodged a bullet. I continued to go in for regular check-ups. I had no choice. If you're diagnosed with cancer, frequent doctor visits are required. They become part of your life. It was one of those check-ups that ultimately saved my life.

In 1981, during a routine check-up, the doctor discovered that the cancer had returned. It was serious. The only hope I had for survival was to have surgery to remove my only remaining vocal chord and larynx. Doing so would mean that I would never talk again. I was devastated. I had been through so much and worked so hard to regain my health. At that moment, I thought I was going to die and that was it. But, all I needed was some time to get over the initial shock and regroup. I needed to prepare to fight the greatest opponent of my life, cancer. I was determined to win this battle, or at least die trying (literally).

The doctors said that if they performed the surgery, and all went well, I would survive. I might even be cancer free, if it hadn't spread to other parts of my body. I actually looked on the bright side and started to feel fortunate. I had a chance. There have been great medical advancements in the treatment of cancer the last few decades. In my day, being diagnosed with cancer was perceived to be a death sentence in most cases. I couldn't help but think about Coach Lombardi. I was lucky, or at least luckier than most diagnosed with cancer. I had a chance. My attitude quickly changed. I was going to live. I might not be able to talk, but I would survive. I was thankful for what I had, not sorry for what I was losing.

Dr. James Brandenberg performed surgery to remove my vocal chords and my larynx. The night before the surgery, Sue and the kids were at my bedside. It would be the last time they would ever hear my voice, at least as they knew it. Truthfully, I was worried about making it. Sue later said that she could see the fear in my eyes and could tell that I was scared. Prior to surgery, I kept telling myself, "You've got your wife, your kids and your spirit. You'll make it work."

I figured the surgery would be painful and the recovery miserable. Unfortunately, I was right on both accounts. Sue was allowed in my room shortly after surgery. Afterwards, she told me there were tubes everywhere, and that I was coughing and in a great deal of pain. She was really upset. What wife wouldn't be?

Even through the pain and commotion, I knew that I was still the same guy. I just couldn't talk. A lot of people can't talk. A lot of people talk too much. I knew I wouldn't have that problem. Not anymore, anyway, and I tried to accept it the best as I could.

When I first returned home after surgery, I tried to write down questions and answers to communicate. I would write out a question to someone and one of two things would happen. They would either write their response, forgetting that I could hear just fine, or start talking really loud, as if I were deaf. I can't help but laugh about it now, but it didn't seem that funny at the time.

It was terrible. It was so slow and boring. I started to work really hard on being able to communicate. I would practice talking in front of the mirror. It was painful both physically and emotionally. I was scheduled to see a speech therapist at the University of Wisconsin-Oshkosh to learn how to talk again. I only went once because I had already started to teach myself.

At first, I couldn't say anything. When I finally got a sound out I felt like celebrating. It took a lot of work. I had to breathe really deep just to get out a sound. I had a robotic microphone, but I hated it. It didn't always work, and when it did, I thought it sounded just awful. So, I kept practicing and praying.

I practiced by trying to say, "Green Bay Packers," or Sue's name, or the kids' names. I did this in front of the mirror in the morning, while I was alone after dinner or while I was driving. I was practicing, and there was wind coming out, but no sound.

One day, while I was alone in my car, a sound came out. Nobody could hear me, and nobody could understand me, but I was talking and it was terrific. I began honking my horn, but nobody in the cars near me could understand why. I remember I was driving to Manitowoc the first time I really got a word out. It was a great feeling to be able to make a sound again.

It was a difficult time because I was at home practicing talking while Sue was at work supporting us. Our roles were reversed. Sue was so helpful in getting me through that difficult time, both emotionally and financially.

I used to be the life of the party. I used to be spontaneous, quick to sing and dance, and I used to talk a lot. All that changed. I still loved to party. I just wasn't very good at it anymore.

The hardest part for me was the alumni reunions, when everyone was talking and reminiscing. I couldn't get a word in edgewise. That bothered me more than anything because I felt like I wasn't part of the group. Nobody could hear me say anything. By the time I could write it on a piece of paper, or everyone got quiet enough to hear me, the moment had passed.

So I'd sit there and try to enjoy hearing my teammates' reminisce. I told my teammates I was feeling fine and didn't want anyone feeling sorry for me. They adjusted to my throat cancer. We never really talked about it. I guess we didn't really have to.

I was glad to be alive, and to have a second chance. I could have drowned in my own self-pity, and almost did for brief moments on really bad days, but I refused to quit. I made a conscious effort to tell myself, "No self pity." I knew that the cancer could have killed me. It was a gift that I was still here, and I wasn't going to waste it feeling sorry for myself. The whole experience made me think about my mortality.

I didn't know what was going to happen to me, but I knew life was going to change. I decided to play it day-by-day, do the best I can, and whatever happens, happens. I didn't know if the cancer would return one final, fatal time, but I did know that if I ever wanted to talk again, it was going to be up to me. I had beaten the odds my whole life, and I was determined to do it one more time.

It all seems like a lifetime ago. Looking back, I can't believe it was 23 years ago that I conquered the biggest challenge of my life, cheated death, and gained even more of an appreciation for life.

At the same time I was trying to beat cancer, I was also battling serious financial problems, including bankruptcy. I went into the restaurant business while we were living in Neenah. Within a few years, I owned a share in eleven thriving bars and supper clubs in Wisconsin, Minnesota and Florida.

It was a great time, and business was booming. The bars and restaurants were grossing between $10 and $15 million a year by the early 1970's. Time magazine did a story on the businesses.

Life was good. The home we owned in Neenah was very nice. We also owned a cottage in northern Wisconsin. We drove nice cars, and our kids were doing great.

Unfortunately, the economy wasn't doing as well. Interest rates skyrocketed from approximately 6 percent to 20 percent. The banks had loaned us the money to expand, and, in time, the payments were too much to handle. With a slowing economy and high unemployment, people didn't have as much discretionary income. I stayed in the business too long and listened to bad advice. In this case, my optimistic nature finally caught up with me.

Although the interest rates were too high to make the payments, it didn't keep me from trying. Each year, we were forced to close some restaurants, hanging on to others in hopes that the economy would improve. The economy did improve, but not in time to save us. I just couldn't keep up with the payments. Eventually, we had to file Chapter 11. At least we managed to pay off our employees.

We lost our house, our cottage, and all but one of our bars. We had to sell our cars. There was no money. It was tough, and it was embarrassing, but we survived. When times are really tough, you learn who your real friends are. I know it's a cliché, but it's true. We scrimped and scraped, and we're thankful for all of the great friends that helped us get through such a tough time. Truthfully, they saved us. I don't know if we could have made it without their help.

Individually, I think either the illness or the financial problems might have torn apart our marriage, but the fact that they happened at the same time may have been a blessing in disguise. Sue and I fought everything together. We were still a team. We knew it would never be great again, but it would be okay. During that most difficult time, Sue and I learned how strong we could be and just how much we loved each other.

A state newspaper did an article on my cancer and our financial troubles.

The reporter interviewed us separately. I told him the reason we survived was because Sue was so strong. Sue told him the only reason we survived was because I was so strong. That's the honest truth. Neither of us knew what the other one said, but we were both on the same page. For a long time, the cancer kept us so busy that the financial problems, as serious as they were, didn't seem as important as trying to stay alive.

I think people with my problems, cancer and finances, were sympathetic to me. They were more patient and forgiving than they otherwise may have been because I kept moving forward and trying to solve the problems. I didn't run from them. I faced them and did my best.

After everything, I still had a passion for the bar and restaurant business. We opened Fuzzy's Steak House in Neenah, but we wanted to get back to Green Bay. We opened Shenanigan's Bar on Riverside Drive in De Pere, just outside of Green Bay. Sue was sweeping the floors, cleaning the bathrooms, and working in the kitchen. I was taking inventory, stocking shelves and running the bar. It wasn't much, but it was ours.

We lost our house of 23 years in Neenah, and our cottage near Antigo, but we weren't bitter. We were appreciative of all the things we did have. Sue could have complained, but she didn't. She was too busy getting in there and doing what needed to be done.

At one time, we had it all, and then we didn't have anything. That was tough on Sue. We both tried to keep our lives as normal as possible, though, and we tried to keep our children away from the financial problems. We didn't want them worrying about something they couldn't control. It wouldn't have been fair to them.

Sue rose to the challenge. She was stronger than I ever knew. We moved to a smaller house in Green Bay. I revived my health and regained my energy, and we began talking about putting our lives back together.

After I was diagnosed with cancer, Sue kept smoking for another ten years before she quit. Oh, she'd quit for a month here or a month there, but it was difficult because she really enjoyed it. I thought she went without smoking once for an entire year. Then, I heard the flick of a lighter in the other room one day, and I knew she'd been smoking the whole time. Finally, on New Year's Day, 1996, the year the Packers won the Super Bowl, she threw away her pack of Merit Ultra Lights and quit smoking for good.

The story has a happy ending. I went for cancer check-ups twice each year for the first five years, but after ten years, my doctor assured me it wouldn't come back. My blood pressure is good, 130 over 65, and I have a good cholesterol number.

Sue and I are owners of Fuzzy's 63 Bar and Fuzzy's Tickets and Tours, both located in Green Bay. We also own a house on the Chain O' Lakes in Waupaca. It has been a long and rewarding road back.

I still get calls from people that have relatives with throat cancer, or who are battling the disease in some other way. It's easy to give advice. I tell those who will lose their vocal chords that they can have a good life. It may be difficult to be understood in a crowded room, but they can carry on a conversation and enjoy people. On occasion, people will call the day before they're having surgery. I try to cheer them up. I tell them it will be okay, and I'm living proof.

I believe that fate plays an important role in life. Many things are simply out of our control. What we can control is how we react to life's adversities and challenges. I believe that the lessons I learned from the role models in my life have helped me to overcome the challenges. My mother always taught me to appreciate what you have, not what you don't have. My wife Sue reinforced that belief during my battles with cancer and bankruptcy.

I believe that my ability to fight and overcome these challenges is also a reflection on Coach Lombardi. He taught me about the will required to persevere through tough times and the discipline required to succeed. Coach Lombardi had a famous saying "The will to win, will to succeed, these are the things that endure". Coach Lombardi was right. He taught me never to quit, and I never will.

Chapter 8
I Love This Bar

Where everyone knows my name - and jersey number

"The only way you can truly understand what I am talking about is to stop by the bar for a visit. Consider this your personal invitation from me..."

"I love this bar, come as you are" is not only in the jukebox, it describes the attitude and atmosphere at Fuzzy's 63 Bar in Green Bay, Wisconsin. You can be a winner or loser, chain smoker or boozer, but you better be a Packers fan.

Fuzzy's 63 Bar can only be described as a Packers shrine in a festive setting. The bar features wall-to-wall pictures of Packers players and national celebrities from Super Bowl I to the present team. Many of the pictures capture the magical moments on and off the field that I enjoyed with my Lombardi era teammates and coaches.

Two of my favorite things are a cold drink and good discussion, especially when the cocktails are on the house and the conversation is with a diehard Packers fan. They go together like green and gold, Hornung and Taylor, Kramer and Thurston. It just wouldn't be right to have one without the other. I can't imagine Vince Lombardi without winning World Championships,

just like I couldn't imagine me not being in the bar business. It gives me a chance to reminisce with the greatest fans in the world.

Through the years, I have always enjoyed going to neighborhood bars. My hometown of Altoona is like many small towns in Wisconsin. It had 1,100 people, 3 bars and no shortage of night life. As a young man, I remember being drawn to those places like a moth to a flame. You drank a few beers, had a few laughs, played some pool and darts, or just shot the breeze.

Of course, there was also the jukebox and dancing. I love to dance and always will. I think it's the secret to my marriage with Sue. Whenever we had a disagreement, I managed to dance my way back into her good graces. After all these years, there is nothing better than a nice slow dance with my wife. It might be a little slower than it used to be, but neither one of us is complaining [wink].

I guess you could say it's in my blood. Not necessarily the drinking, although I've knocked back a few in my time, but I must admit an addiction to dancing, socializing and singing my favorite Frank Sinatra or Louis Armstrong song on karaoke night.

Back in the 60's, I loved to go out with my teammates after the game. I wanted us to be able to go to a place where we could be close to the fans and each other. Thus, I decided to open my own bar and restaurant. In those days, we didn't make the kind of money that today's players earn. In fact, we were just like the fans, trying to put food on the table. We may have been more recognizable, but we didn't consider ourselves any better or different. We didn't want to sneak in the back room to avoid the fans after the game. We partied WITH them. To this day, I still have that mentality.

Years ago, I met a fellow named Mal Kennedy of Madison. He was a big fan of the Wisconsin Badgers and Green Bay Packers. He and I became friends, and one night I told him I would like to get into the bar and restaurant business. I loved people, especially Packers fans, and it was a way to stay close to them and earn a living at the same time.

Fuzzy and Forrest Gregg out on the town.

Mal put me in touch with a gentleman named Bill Martine, a great chef, who also had an interest in the bar and restaurant business. Bill and I hit it off right away, and that is how I came to open my first supper club, The Left Guard, in Menasha in 1961. We had

Max McGee and Fuzzy sing karaoke at Fuzzy's 63.

great food and a nice little bar with a restaurant that could seat 50. A year or two later, we remodeled the upstairs and doubled the seating capacity.

In 1965, we brought in Max McGee as a partner and expanded throughout the state. We opened a Left End in Manitowoc, and another Left Guard in Appleton. We expanded to Minneapolis, Eau Claire, Madison, Janesville, Fond du Lac, Milwaukee, Green Bay and Miami, Florida. My bars were THE place for my teammates to go every Sunday after the game and Monday on our day off. The players and fans would sing, dance, shoot dice and have a few beers. It was a great way to unwind before practice started on Tuesday.

At first, the business really flourished. Perhaps I expanded too fast, and eventually things got really tough. I was forced to close the bars. In hind-site, I wouldn't change anything because I didn't go into the restaurant business to make millions. I wanted to make friends, have fun with my teammates and connect with the fans. If I didn't have a bar all these years, where the hell would everyone go? I don't even like to think about it because we had so much fun.

Sue and I decided to own and operate just one bar and restaurant. We opened Fuzzy's Steakhouse in Neenah, but our heart was in Green Bay. Soon afterward, we leased a bar in Green Bay called Shenanigans. Sue's mother always said that the name was perfect to describe the behavior of the players in the bar. It was small, but it was ours. Once again, we enjoyed the interaction between the players and the fans. As our business expanded, so did our need for a bigger place. Eventually, we found a home on the west side of Green Bay, opening Fuzzy's 63 Bar, where we currently own and operate.

People ask me why I still want to own a bar at 72 years of age. Why? Because it's still fun. I may not be as young as I used to be, but the night's always young when I'm doing what I love, having a good old-fashioned discussion

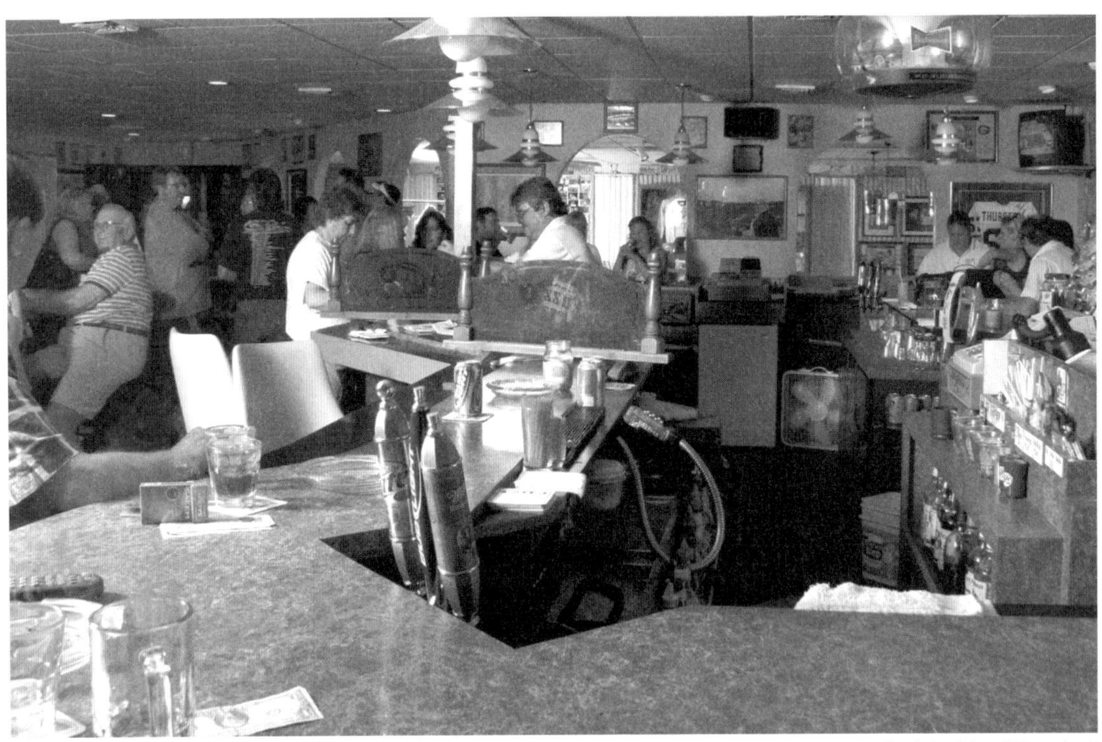

A look inside of Fuzzy's 63

about the Packers. It's the main reason I opened a bar and restaurant in the first place, and that hasn't changed. In all honesty, I never imagined that, after all these years, I would still own a tavern, be surrounded by Packers fans, and be enjoying every moment of it. Most of the time, there is no place on earth I would rather be.

The minute you enter Fuzzy's 63, you will feel as if you've stepped back in time. There are hundreds of photos, including pictures of me with former teammates and national celebrities such as Gerald Ford, Mickey Mantle, Lee Trevino and Meat Loaf, to name a few. The bar is lined with Packers themed license plates from virtually every state in the country.

Several of my employees have been with me for many years and are on a first-name basis with both the locals and Packers fans from around the country. Joan has been with me for over twenty years and was with me when we started Shenanigans. Kay started at Shenanigans more than fifteen years ago, right around the time my wife, Sue, quit the bar. Now, when you stop by my bar, you can count on them entertaining you with great stories from the past. Packers' home game weekends are like reunions for customers and staff alike. I believe in great customer service and making people feel welcome, so I know you're sure to enjoy talking Packers football with the entire staff at Fuzzy's 63.

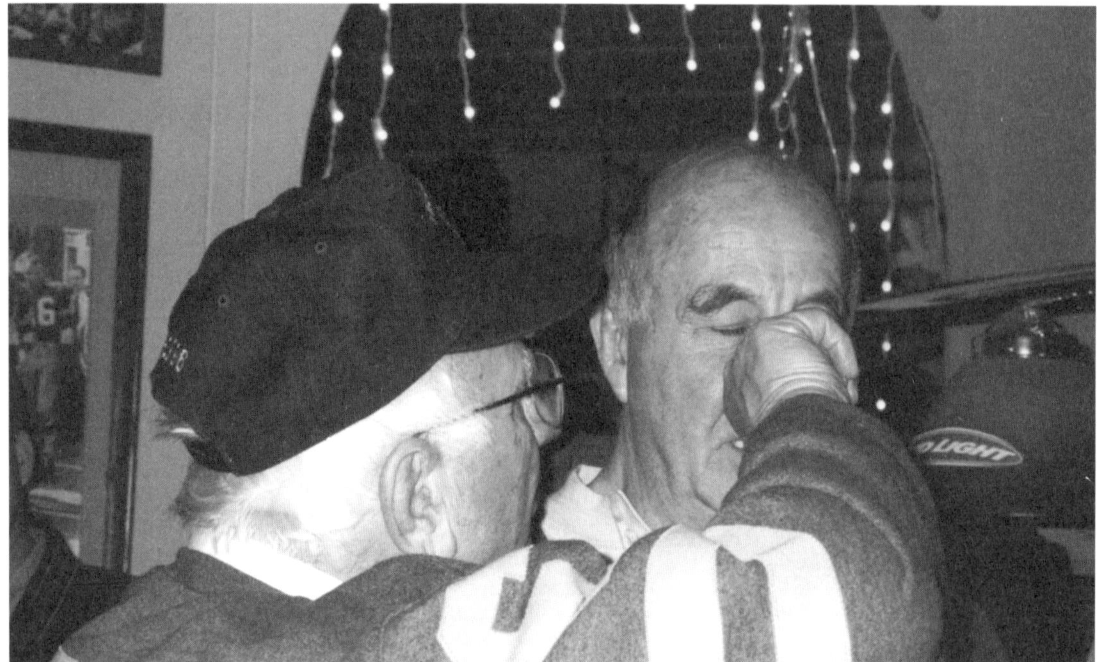

Clowning around with Max McGee.

I hang out at the bar on Packers weekends and autograph Fuzzy's 63 merchandise and photos. Fans stop by the bar to take a walk down memory lane, hang with me and some of my teammates, and get fired up for the game. It is great to see old faces, but nothing is more exciting than seeing the look on the face of a Packers fan making their first "pilgrimage" to Lambeau Field. Some have tears in their eyes they're so emotional. Some bring their sons, daughters or grandkids, to continue the family tradition. It helps me feel young, and it's a reminder of just how special it is to attend a Packers game in Titletown, USA. I don't ever want to take that feeling for granted. To be honest, I'm not sure who's having a better time – the customers or me.

The bar is packed on Saturday and Sunday nights of a Packers home game weekend. On any given night, don't be surprised to see me take the microphone to sing my favorite song, Louis Armstrong's "What a Wonderful World." It's no coincidence that it's also the title of this book. I end every song with "God bless the Green Bay Packers." I have also been known to take to the dance floor, especially when there is a good Frank Sinatra tune playing. My personal favorites are "My Way" and "Summer Wind." The only way you can truly understand what I am talking about is to stop by the bar for a visit. Consider this your personal invitation from me, not that you need one. Everyone is always welcome at Fuzzy's 63 Bar.

Boyd Dowler having some fun at Fuzzy's place on a Packers game weekend.

The people I've met, the pictures I've taken and had taken, and the autographs I've signed mean a lot to me. I have never turned down an autograph request. I think fans respect and even admire me for that. It's one of the reasons I have such a great relationship with Packers fans.

We've had a lot of memorable moments in my bars. I've seen newlyweds come in right after the ceremony to have their picture taken with the bridal party. I've seen fans that haven't been to a Packers game in years, but came back just to see if good old Fuzzy, or Paul, or Max might be around the bar.

Whenever my former teammates come to Green Bay, the first stop on their itinerary is my place. On Alumni weekend, it's typical to have as many as twenty former players in the bar at one time, all signing autographs and talking football with the patrons. It's kind of the meeting place for former Packers. I take a great deal of pride in the

L to R: Ron Kramer, Fuzzy Thurston and Willie Wood.

fact that former players think enough of me to stop by, shake hands, and sign autographs for my customers. I like being the guy that can provide a place for fans and players to meet each other.

I'm also in the Packers ticket and tour business. In my opinion, these two businesses go hand-in-hand. Visiting the bar is a great time, but every football fan, no matter what their team allegiance, MUST attend a Packers home game. There's no better place in America to watch a football game, and there is definitely no better place to tailgate before the game. The morning of a game, you can see tents with smoke billowing from grills throughout the stadium area. You can smell the bratwurst from miles away. Everyone and everything is draped in green and gold. Fans come from all around the world for this unique experience.

Currently, I'm one of the largest season ticket holders of the Green Bay Packers, with approximately 200 season tickets per game. This didn't happen by accident. After each of my early seasons with the Packers, Coach

Lombardi offered me the choice of a cash raise or an opportunity to purchase season tickets. I decided to take the season tickets. Coach Lombardi was not surprised because he knew just how much I loved the Green Bay Packers.

The same can't be said for a couple of my teammates. Max McGee and Paul Hornung are very successful businessmen. Whatever they touch seems to turn to gold. Contrary to what they may modestly tell you, it isn't just because they're lucky. They're two of the smartest, shrewdest, and fairest businessmen you will ever meet.

That's why I'm especially proud of the fact that I decided to take the season tickets. I remember Paul and Max both telling me, "Take the money. Those tickets are worth a lot right now, but after we're done playing, and if the team isn't winning, they're not going to be worth

L to R: Max McGee, Fuzzy Thurston and Paul Hornung.

anything."

When they said that, I remember thinking, "Uh-oh. Maybe I screwed up." But, I knew how important tickets were for the bar business. Packers' fans wanted to come to my place to party before the game and celebrate or commiserate afterwards. I thought about the Packers' great tradition and rich history. I was confident that those tickets would have tremendous value for a long, long time. In addition to their value to my business, it would keep me close to the fans, which was my major motivation. It would also be a good way to stay involved with the team after I retired.

There were a lot of lean years, of course, and for a while I thought maybe Paul and Max were right. Some of those years in the 1970's and 1980's, nobody wanted tickets to the game. I used to give away many of my tickets to good customers and hope to sell the rest for face value.

I wasn't making any money, but I wasn't worried. I always figured better days were ahead. I'm an optimist, especially where the Packers are concerned. I figured they'd have a winner sooner than later.

I was right! The Packers fortunes quickly turned for the better in the early 90's with the arrival of Bob Harlan, Ron Wolf, Mike Holmgren, Brett Favre, Reggie White and a cast of talented players. Tickets were in demand, and everybody in town was my best friend again.

I still tease Max and Paul about my decision to this day. I might be the only person that actually went against their business advice with no regrets.

In addition to the Packers winning, I also was fortunate enough to meet Bill Wenzel, my good friend and current business partner. In the late 1980's, Bill owned a sports tours company in Chicago and desperately needed game

Fuzzy with his longtime friend and business partner Bill Wenzel. L to R: Ben Stone, Bill Wenzel, Fuzzy and Griff Thurston.

tickets for the Bears game in Green Bay. Even though Bill is a diehard Packers fan, he was running tours for Bears fans to Green Bay. I thought it was a tough way for a Packers fan to make a buck, especially considering the success of the Chicago Bears in the mid to late 1980's. At the time, it looked like the Packers might never beat the Bears again. As we all know, things changed in the 90's, and the Packers have dominated the Bears in recent history.

Bill placed a classified ad in the Green Bay Press-Gazette looking to buy tickets for the Packers-Bears game at Lambeau Field. I called Bill, and I remember him telling me that he was in the middle of his fantasy football draft when his mother came downstairs and said, "Someone named Fuzzy is on the telephone and he wants to speak with you." Bill said his friends just looked at him in awe. Even Bears fans knew there was only one Fuzzy, THE FUZZY, and he was waiting on the telephone. I could tell immediately that Bill loved the Green Bay Packers. He was so excited to talk with me, telling me I was a boyhood idol. He almost forgot to ask about the tickets. My response to that ad was the beginning of an amazing friendship.

Bill and I became friends quickly, and for about three or four years I sold him my Bears tickets, which was always the hottest ticket in town. Finally, I told Bill that I couldn't just sell him the Bears game. I asked if he might be interested in buying the entire season-ticket package, rather than just the one game. I remember Bill agonizing over his decision for days before finally buying the tickets for the entire season. Bill and I have a good laugh about it, even today. What turned out to be a stroke of genius was actually a tough decision, but it was the right decision.

That led to Bill starting a Packers Tour Company, which later became the Official Tour Company of the Green Bay Packers. Bill hired me to sign autographs at the welcome receptions for a number of years. Eventually, Bill moved from Chicago to Green Bay, sold his tour company, and is my current partner with Fuzzy's Tickets and Tours. Bill has worked in the sports tour business for over twenty years. We make a great team. I feel good knowing that if anything were to happen to me, Bill will continue the tradition I started.

It's still hard to believe that the decision to acquire Packers tickets from Vince Lombardi and a phone call to a stranger that placed a classified ad would result in a very successful Packers ticket and tour business. I feel blessed to have the opportunity to provide Packers fans from any destination with the experience I love so much - attending a Packers' game and a good old-fashioned Wisconsin tailgate party.

Chapter 9
TITLETOWN AGAIN!
The Lombardi Trophy Comes Home

"It was almost 30 years since I had helped the Packers win the first Super Bowl, but for that moment it seemed like yesterday."

I was standing on the 15 yard-line, feeling like I was 25 years old again. Lambeau Field, one of the most beautiful places on Earth, was jumping like I hadn't seen it since I was a much younger man and the Packers were a dominant team.

The Packers had just finished their most amazing comeback in years. Brett Favre threw a touchdown pass with only a few seconds to play and we stunned the Cincinnati Bengals, 24-23, in front of a packed house. I was thrilled for the Packers, and I was thrilled for me, because the Packers had won on one of my favorite days of the season, Alumni Day.

That day wasn't just a reunion, though. It was a rebirth. It was the fall of 1992, Alumni weekend. The Packers were recovering from a 4-12 season in 1991, and I was recovering from hip-replacement surgery. I walked with a limp and a cane, but I felt like the Packers and their new coach, Mike

Holmgren, were moving in the right direction.

Alumni weekend is very special to me. It is a reunion of former Packers players from every decade. For me, it is a rare chance to visit with many of my teammates. I only see some of them once a year, on Alumni weekend. One of the best things about Alumni Day is getting to stand on

Fuzzy is introduced at half-time on Alumni Weekend to a sold-out crowd at Lambeau Field.

the sidelines, being announced to the crowd at half-time, and watching the game with all those great former Packers players. It is always exciting, and this game was especially so.

When the Packers won, I couldn't contain myself. I limped onto the field and headed straight for the 50 yard-line, but I settled for the 15. I just stood there, soaking in the sights and sounds, and it seemed like the celebration would last forever.

After twenty minutes or so, the players, current and past, had already made their way through the tunnel and into the locker room. Not me. I just stood there, and really not knowing why, I began thrusting my cane into the air. The more I smiled and thrust that cane skyward, the louder the fans cheered. I felt like Leonard Bernstein conducting his orchestra to the sweetest song of all. I felt like the Packers might be back after all.

Plus, I'm a ham. I can't help it. I love the Packers so much, and the fans even more, that I get caught up in the moment. I thought, "What the heck." My Packers were showing signs of life, and this come-from-behind win over the Bengals was just the beginning of big things to come. I felt that way, and I think the fans felt that way, too.

Green Bay Packers Head Coach Mike Homgren (1992-1998) and Fuzzy

I was happy to see Ron Wolf, the terrific, no-nonsense general manager, make a change and bring in Holmgren to be the head coach. Holmgren was a winner in San Francisco, and I figured he'd be a winner here, too.

I liked Holmgren a lot, and I liked him right away. But, I was also cautious. I am a real excitable guy, and we had been through so many bad years, I didn't want to get my hopes up too high. I wanted to see Mike do something first, and that he did. He got better every year, and his teams got better every year, too.

It was the same with Brett Favre. I was impressed with the way he could move, and that he could throw the ball a mile. He had a rocket for an arm, and he was tough, daring, and fun loving. I liked him right away, and I

Fuzzy and his great friend Brett Favre.

thought he would have been a great teammate. I also thought he would have fit right in with our great teams of the 1960's.

I'm not the only Thurston that thought so. There is a very good reason why I am Brett's second-biggest fan. That is because my wife is his No. 1 fan. When he throws a touchdown pass, Sue goes nuts. When he throws an interception, she can't bear to watch. Sue would adopt Brett if she could. I know this because she has been saying it for the past 15 years.

When Brett led the Packers' upset of Cincinnati, I remember thinking that maybe this was the guy that would take us back to the Super Bowl.

Now, I was a big Don Majkowski fan. Sue and I were good friends with him. We went to his wedding. He was a really good quarterback, but that shoulder injury kind of did him in. I remember feeling bad for Don because he was such a good kid, a good man.

But as a Packers fan you hoped and prayed that the best was still to come. And it was. When we were losing, it was very, very difficult to accept. As a die-hard Packers fan, those were tough years. All you could do was hope for the best, and then wait until next year. For a while, it seemed like next year would never come.

Back in the 1970s and 1980s, we would get excited if the Packers made the ESPN highlights. We would be at my tavern, Shenanigan's, and we would cheer and celebrate for the Packers. We had great times, and when they won, it really got crazy.

The Packers just kept getting better under Wolf, Holmgren and Brett. When Reggie White signed here in the spring of 1993, I was tickled. I knew that it was a big step. We needed help defensively to get where we needed to be, and

Reggie White, the Minister of Defense. in Super Bowl X

I didn't have any doubts about Reggie White. He was the greatest defensive player in the game, and he was ours.

Sue and I were in Florida when the Packers signed Reggie in free agency, and it was so exciting that our daughter, Tori, held the telephone up to the TV so we could hear the live broadcast of the local news conference. I got shivers just watching Sue listen.

Everybody thought we were getting better, that we were on the move, and it was fun again. The bar business kept getting better and better, too. The ticket business was booming, people wanted to go again, and I couldn't have been prouder. The whole ride was exciting.

I'll never forget the day the Packers' defense held the Lions' Barry Sanders to negative yards. It was in 1994 – the NFC Wild Card Game at Lambeau Field – and the Packers won, 16-12. Sanders, one of the greatest backs I've ever seen, just couldn't do anything against the Packers' defense. Wasn't he just the greatest runner to watch? Especially when the Packers were smothering him?

That season didn't start out so great, though. The night before the '94 season opener Sterling Sharpe, the talented receiver, threatened to hold out if the Packers didn't give him a new contract. I was pissed. This never would have happened in my playing days. Coach Lombardi would not have allowed it to get to that point. I was so upset with Sharpe for holding out. I was very disappointed. How could he do that? I heard the news on the radio while I was driving to Shenanigan's, and I thought, "How could he do that? Does he think he's bigger than the Packers?"

What I did like was the fact that Brett came out and publicly said he disagreed with Sterling's stunt, but that he would re-do his own contract if it meant Sharpe would play. Now there's a leader. Then, Brett went out and threw the game-winning touchdown pass to Sterling and the Packers won, 16-10. It was a great win over a division rival, and I was happy for Holmgren and Brett, but I never liked Sharpe after that.

Luckily, the good times far outweighed the bad in the coming years. Sue still talks about the Christmas Eve game the next year. The Packers beat the Pittsburgh Steelers, 24-19, when Yancey Thigpen dropped an easy touchdown pass in the closing seconds of the game. What a Christmas gift.

When the pass was in the air, and Sue saw the Steelers' receiver all alone in the back of the end zone, she put her head in her hands. She never saw Thigpen drop it. Our son, Griff, poked her in the side and shouted, "He dropped it!" Then the crowd went wild and it was just bedlam.

There were other highlights, too. In 1995, I got to celebrate one of my favorite national holidays, my birthday, with Frankie Winters, Mark Chmura and Brett Favre. They came into Shenanigan's and all the kids and grandkids and I had our picture taken with them. It was funny because the grandkids were running around and having fun and racing through the bar, and then all of a sudden they came to a screeching halt. That was when Brett walked in. The grandkids blinked and never said another word until he left. They were in awe. Brett was just Brett. He joked around, as did his pals, and it was a great time. I still have the pictures on the fireplace mantle at our home in Waupaca, Wisconsin.

Sue always went to the games, and she always sat on the 48-yard line in section 18. They were terrific seats, and the people that sat near her through the years were just as wonderful. She always says she'll never forget the game – and it was pretty early in the 1990s – when a young father and his son sat near her. Before the game, the father tells his son, "That's No. 4. You're

Fuzzy celebrates his birthday with his friends. L to R, '96 Packers Center Frank Winters , Quarterback Brett Favre, Fuzzy and Tight End Mark Chmura

watching a quarterback that is going to be a legend. I want you to watch this, and to remember it, because there's not going to be another one like Brett Favre around here for a long, long time." Sue said she had never thought about that before, and she never forgot about it since, because that man was right.

In the fall of '96, we moved into our lake home in Waupaca, an hour west of Green Bay. One day after we were moving some things, and the Packers' record was something like 4-1, we talked about, "What if? What if the Packers get to the Super Bowl?" It wasn't anything we dwelled on because it seemed like only a dream. Well, I got talking, and I said, "If we make it to the Super Bowl in New Orleans, I'll take the whole family." One of our son Mark's friends, Gazzoo, was sitting there. And I looked at him and said I would take him, too.

It seemed like a lot of big talk at the time, but the Packers kept winning and winning, and pretty soon we were thinking, "They just might do it."

The Packers' record improved to 6-1 at the bye weekend, and the national media was beginning to take notice. Things were jumping at Shenanigan's and everything seemed so right. Like I said, I'm a real excitable guy, but I also lived through cancer, bankruptcy and other unpleasantness of life. This was a great feeling and I was going to enjoy the ride. I wanted to share the Packers' run with my entire family, including my in-laws.

You hear comedians make jokes about having to deal with the in-laws. I always smile when I hear that because my in-laws were the greatest people you could imagine.

L to R: Fuzzy and Sue with Sue's parents Lila and Gordie Eggelston.

Gordon "Gordie" Eggleston and his wife Lila weren't just my in-laws. They were my friends. Sue and I did everything with them. We played cards together. We watched sports together. After I retired, we went to all the games together.

I felt especially close to Gordie, Sue's dad, who was a very special guy. I became very close to him. Part of it was because he was such a great guy, and part of it was because I had lost my own father when I was four years old. Gordie was like a father to me.

Now, Gordie was a Packers fan, and he had a son-in-law that played for the Packers' championship teams of the 1960s. He loved that. He was always so proud. Gordie and I grew close through the years, and when the Packers began to win again in the 1990s it was great. I don't think we talked about the Packers going back to the Super Bowl in 1996, but I knew Gordie was hoping they would get there. That's why it was so tough when we lost him.

It was the Wednesday after the Packers' bye weekend when we got a phone call. Gordie had died in his sleep. The covers weren't even messed up. If only all of us could go so peacefully. He was so warm and so good, and he was such a big part of my life that I can't tell you how difficult that was for me. Of course, it was even harder on Sue. Gordie was 87 when he passed away.

Sue felt so bad that her dad never knew the Packers went back to the Super Bowl, but I told her, "He knew, Sue. He knew."

It wasn't easy, but we had to get on with our lives, and the Packers' winning season was definitely a tremendous diversion.

The Packers kept playing so well, and by the time they qualified for the playoffs, we were confident they were going to get to Super Bowl XXXI. First, they had to get past the Carolina Panthers in the NFC Championship game at Lambeau Field. Some fans might have been nervous, but I wasn't worried. I never worry. I'm the eternal optimist. I just felt that with the fans and Brett and the cold weather it was going to be impossible for Carolina to beat the Packers.

The night before the game we had a great party at Shenanigan's. It was so jammed you couldn't even move. Pam Oliver, a reporter from ESPN, was there. So was Jim Rome. I really liked Jim. He was enthusiastic and he never stopped talking. He was going 90 miles an hour. He made the evening so much fun for everyone there.

Fuzzy's bar - always the place to be on Packers game weeke

So did one of Donny Anderson's good friends from Texas. Donny was in town for the game, and he and his buddy stopped in to Shenanigan's probably around 10 o'clock. Donny's friend said he would like to buy drinks for the bar. I thought he meant a round. He meant he'd like to buy the drinks until closing time. The tab came to something like $13,000 – if that gives you an idea of how much fun we had – and the Texan didn't even bat an eye. He just smiled and paid in cash.

The next morning I was up at 7 o'clock and heading over to Shenanigan's to take care of the tickets and the tailgaters and the busses. Finally it was game time, and we played so well it was fabulous. The Packers defeated Carolina, 30-13, and the feeling at Lambeau Field was electric. It was one of the great days of my life.

Sue, Fuzzy and their son Mark arrive at the Superdome in Orleans for Super Bowl X

Then, it was off to New Orleans for Super Bowl XXXI. We were there from Thursday through Sunday, just Sue and me and our kids and Mark's friend. What a great time. Sue and I had been one of the hosts for the

Fuzzy and Sue in the stands at Super Bowl XXXI cheering on the Pack.

"Taste of the NFL" party they hold each year. It involved a golf tournament, a party and some of the best food from around the country.

Afterward, Sue and I went back to our hotel to have a little R&R. It wasn't long before there was a knock on our hotel door. I opened the door and a man was standing there in Green Bay Packers' clothes. He smiled at me, put his hand in his shirt pocket and said, "I know who you are and you've got money. I've got a gun and I want some of it. NOW!"

Just about then Sue figured out something was wrong and she began to ask who was at the door. I just motioned her back with one hand while I reached into my pants pocket with the other. I pulled out $25 and gave it to him. I wasn't going to take any chances with Sue in the room, and even under his jacket, the gun seemed real enough.

I said, "All I've got is $25, but I'll have more tomorrow."

Brett Favre and Reggie White celebrating after the w

He took the money, turned and walked away down the hallway. He didn't even run. He wasn't worried at all. I was just relieved to see him go, and I was wondering, "How stupid can I be? I'll have MORE money tomorrow?" I was just glad we never saw him again. Aside from the "gun incident" as it is known in the Thurston household, we went ahead and had a great time in New Orleans.

What I remember most was the start of the game, when Brett called an audible, faked a handoff to Edgar Bennett and hit Andre Rison for the first touchdown of the game. Brett went nuts and he pulled his helmet off and began running around the field. I never saw a guy more excited. Right then I thought, "This is going to be a great day for Green Bay."

It was such a great relief to me. I was so down for so many years, and I thought, "God, I've waited so long for this. Thank you." I was so happy for the team, and I know Green Bay fans wanted another Super Bowl so badly, and then it happened. It thrilled me to death. It was just like I was playing again. It was wonderful.

When they sang the National Anthem before the kickoff, I looked around and there were tears coming down on the faces of Packers fans around us. Those tears of joy returned when the Packers beat the New England Patriots, 35-21, and the party was on.

Great friends Jerry Kramer, Dick Schaap and Fuzzy Thurston.

After the game, Sue ran into our good friend Dick Schaap. Dick was a sports writer, ESPN commentator and author of "Instant Replay" and other Packers related books. Dick was also a huge Packers fan. As Sue gave Dick a hug, he whispered in her ear, "We finally made it back." Dick always said he loved three sports teams in his life, but the Green Bay Packers was the only team that loved him back. I can tell you that my teammates and I certainly loved Schaap.

The next day, we drove to Brett Favre's hometown, Kiln, Mississippi, and we were just exhausted. We were mentally and physically drained, but we wanted to see where Brett grew up. It was so surreal. We were sitting in the Broke Spoke, a bar that Brett Favre frequented, watching the victory parade in Green Bay on TV. I'll never forget it.

For me, I had forgotten how great it felt to win a Super Bowl. On this day, all of the feelings, pride and emotion of winning a championship came flooding back again. It was almost 30 years since I had helped the Packers win the first Super Bowl, but for that moment it seemed like yesterday. I felt young again.

I often get asked which team was better. The teams I played on or the 1996 Super Bowl XXXI team?

I think that's tough to compare because it was different players from different eras. They had tremendous athletes, as did we, but we were able to stay together for so many years. That was one of the reasons why we very seldom made mental mistakes. The other was Coach Lombardi.

I will say this. I thought that 1996 team was as good as we were, but if we played them, I think we would have beaten them.

Chapter 10
Glory Years to Golden Years

"It's true that nothing lasts forever, unless it's a person's attitude towards life."

Whenever I run into somebody I haven't seen in a long time, they always ask, "How are you doing, Fuzzy?" Great, I say, and it's true. Sure, I wish I was thirty again, and it was 1963, and I was the starting left guard on the Green Bay Packers' World Championship team. Don't we all?

Those were great times and great teams, and the Packers were THE No. 1 team in American sports culture. But, I don't long for the past, or wish to live in it. I celebrate it. I look back and I think, "What a wonderful world." I look ahead and I feel exactly the same way.

It's true that nothing lasts forever, unless it's a person's attitude toward life. There's so much we can't control, but one thing we can control is our outlook. I'm not always happy with the way things are. Nobody is. That doesn't stop me from choosing to look on the bright side, or trying to find the good in people, or making a conscious effort to focus on the positive rather than dwell on the negative. There is so much to be thankful for.

Sue and I have had our share of health issues and financial problems. When I was diagnosed with cancer I wasn't sure I would live long enough to retire. That was the harsh reality, but it also put things in perspective. At that point, I wasn't worrying about whether I would be able to afford to retire. If you're dead, it doesn't matter, and if you don't appreciate what you have while you're alive, what's the use?

It's why I try to not take anything for granted, beginning with the fact that Green Bay Packers fans are the greatest fans in the world. To me, one of the best aspects of being retired from football is the opportunity it gives me to more time to spend with the fans. I never refuse an autograph request, and I enjoy talking football with fans at Fuzzy's 63 Bar. I realize how lucky I am, and how much I owe to the fans that stop in and say hello. We've had great support from family, friends and all of our customers at Fuzzy's 63 Bar and Fuzzy's Tickets and Tours.

Sue and I have been married nearly fifty years. Anyone married as long as we have knows it isn't easy. Marriage is hard work. Sue has had to endure more worrying, wondering, and late-night clock watching than she cares to remember. She knew I was a party guy, or whatever, and that would irritate her at times. She was often at home while I was out being Fuzzy.

I had a reputation with my teammates for being the life of the party. Whether I was celebrating with the party boys, Hornung, McGee and Ron Kramer after a big win, or commiserating after an especially tough defeat, my heart was always in the right place. Many of my teammates, whom Sue loves like brothers, dubbed her with the nickname Saint Sue. There were times that Sue would get upset with me, but she always knew that I loved her. If she didn't, I don't know how we would have made it all of these years.

For years, Sue and I did everything with her parents. We played cards often, euchre and dirty clubs. When I played on the road, Sue would watch the games on television with her parents. More often than not, we would have a victory to celebrate. That tradition continued after I retired, and Sue and I would watch the away games with her parents. There was always a log burning in the fireplace and a meal in the oven. Unfortunately, there wasn't always a victory to celebrate, but we had fun anyway.

Currently, Sue and I live in a very nice home in Waupaca, located on the Chain O' Lakes. We have a wonderful view of Nessling Lake from our deck. The Fourth of July, with the fireworks and boat parade, is one of our favorite holidays.

The Thurstons' home in Waupaca, Wisconsin

We moved to Waupaca during the Packers' bye week in 1996. We had friends that lived on the Chain O' Lakes. While visiting, we liked it so much we decided to move there. We were living in a duplex in Green Bay, but really wanted to be on the lake.

We have always enjoyed living on the water. When the kids were growing up we had a cottage between Antigo and Rhinelander on Clear Lake. We would spend the summers there. Mark, Griff and Tori would bring their friends, and Sue's parents would visit us. Those were great times. Our children's friends still talk about how much fun they had at our place. Sue would take our kids and their friends swimming, boating, or drive the boat while they were water skiing.

It was a small lake, which suited our needs, because Sue could keep a close eye on the kids from the cottage. Now, our place in Waupaca is perfect because it's a bit secluded and has many lakes. We have just enough privacy, and we don't need to worry about watching the kids to make sure they don't drown. I guess you could say we were in the right cottages at the right times.

Late afternoons, Sue and I like to sip cocktails on the deck and watch the world go by. We also like to go for a ride on the pontoon boat, but don't do it as often as we used to. Sue's knees aren't the best, and if it's just the two of us, it makes docking the boat pretty difficult. We don't entertain as often as we used to, or as often as we'd like to, but when we do, it's great fun.

L to R: Longtime friends Bob and Shirley Thompson enjoying a night with the Thurstons at Fuzzy's bar.

Bob and Shirley Thompson, our longtime best friends from Altoona, visit at least once a year. We have known them since before we were married. Bob and I have been friends since grade school, and Shirley and I met in high school. Bob and Shirley were the best man and maid of honor at our wedding – almost fifty years ago! We're very lucky to have another couple, with whom we get along so well, to share our life.

Of course, we adore our grandchildren and absolutely love when they visit. We have Olivia, who is 22, Freddy, who is 20, and Joey, who is 15. It's always a treat when they visit because we get to spoil them rotten, like grandparents should. The only problem is they don't visit as often anymore because so much is going on in their own lives. I woke up one day, looked at Sue and said, "When did we get so old? And when did the grandchildren get all grown up?" It happens.

We still manage to keep busy, though. Some days it seems like we're busier now than when I was playing and Sue was raising the kids. Sue loves to read and has more than a thousand books in her personal collection. She reads everything from murder mysteries to sports autobiographies, and I'm pretty sure she's read every book every written about the Packers.

She's also on the Internet constantly. She's either reading her email, keeping up with the day's news, or searching for one thing or another. She does crossword puzzles, needlepoint, and takes immaculate care of her flowers, too. Our deck is covered with flowers, and there are several beds in the yard. It's nice because I don't have to water or care for them. All I have to do is sit back and enjoy the view.

Sue adores her cats, Bailey and Beasley, and treats them like royalty. They have warmed up to me, or maybe the other way around, through the years. Every once in awhile Bailey will sit on my lap and catch a catnap, but Beasley steers clear of me. They're good company for Sue while I'm out of town.

The Packers are my hobby. I follow them very closely and watch everything they do. The drafts, the trades, the coaching, I watch sports all the time.

I like to watch golf on television, and I'm a big Phil Mickelson fan. I also like to watch Wisconsin Badgers football and basketball games. I follow the Milwaukee Brewers, and I want them to win. I check the newspaper daily for standings and scores, but the game of baseball is too slow for me to watch.

I travel to Green Bay at least once a week during the spring, summer, and early fall. I get updates on the businesses, run errands, and grab dinner and a room at a nearby hotel. Green Bay is about an hour drive from Waupaca. I typically hang around the bar to listen to karaoke and visit with fans. During the football season, I'm at the bar on Saturday and Sunday of every home game weekend. I enjoy meeting all the fans and signing autographs.

Sue doesn't get to Green Bay as much as she used to because of knee problems. She can't get around like she once did, and the pleasure isn't always worth the pain. Neither of us can believe she was the one that ended up with bad knees, even after I played professional football.

I had both hips replaced in the early 1990's, and they're still good as new. I didn't want to have the surgery, but the pain got to be so bad it was affecting my sleep. Finally, I couldn't take it anymore and agreed to have the replacement surgery. My only regret is that I waited so long.

Otherwise, I feel great. I weigh 265 pounds, which was my playing weight, and I exercise 3-4 times per week. I'm an early riser, so I'm usually on my stationary bicycle by 7 a.m. I'll watch the news, listen to the radio or read the newspaper while I'm peddling for a couple of hours. Some days I hate it, and riding that bike is the last thing I want to do. But, I know it's good for me, so I stick with it.

I've lost about sixty pounds since the mid-1980s. I weighed about 320 pounds at the time my Left Guard restaurants were struggling. I knew I had to make some lifestyle changes, or I wouldn't be around to see my grandkids grow up. When I was diagnosed with cancer, I had to make changes whether I liked it or not. After the cancer surgery, I started exercising regularly and began losing weight.

Packer alumni gather together at the Packer Hall of Fame.
Top Row, L to R: Ken Bowman, Boyd Dowler, Jimmy Taylor, Willie Wood and Willie Davis.
Bottom Row, L to R: Jan Stenerud, Fuzzy Thurston, Ron Wolf, Max McGee, Jerry Kramer and Ray Nitschke.

In 1984, I helped organize a Super Bowl I reunion. At the time, the Packers were one of the few NFL teams that won a Super Bowl to not have a reunion. I remember friends John Fabry and Milt Simons, along with Jackie and Ray Nitschke, and Sue and I getting together to plan the event. That was in early April. On August 26, 1984, I mailed a letter inviting all of my former teammates from the Super Bowl I team to a reunion in Green Bay.

It had been many years since I'd seen some of my teammates. I thought it was about time we had an event where we all got together and had a good time. It needed to be done before we were too old. I did whatever I could to get all my teammates to attend. I made phone calls, I sent letters, I wanted to make it something good, something special, and I wanted to include everyone. The turnout was exceptional.

Jerry Kramer and Dick Schaap used the reunion as the basis for their book, "Distant Replay," which was the follow-up to their bestseller, "Instant Replay." The book was as big a hit as the reunion.

We scheduled the reunion to coincide with the Packers' Alumni Weekend, and I can't remember if we won or lost, but it wasn't the most important thing on our minds. We were happy to be together again. It was a big success.

I had a close relationship with a lot of players, and I didn't want to wait too long to see them. Before the reunion, the only time I'd see my teammates is if they came to town and stopped at Shenanigan's. It's the same way now at Fuzzy's 63 Bar.

I often get asked what Coach Lombardi would think of his former players. My personal feeling is that Coach Lombardi was awfully proud of his players on the championship teams, and he would be even prouder thirty years later. We had a great deal of love and respect for each other as teammates and friends. Those same feelings remain to this day. Many of my former teammates have gone on to become very successful businessmen and exceptional human beings.

Nothing can replace the thrill of running through the tunnel on game day, but being inducted into the Green Bay Packers Hall of Fame comes close. Of all the awards I've won and the honors I've received, being part of that incredible Class of 1975 is the most unbelievable tribute possible.

The Class of 1975 featured Don Chandler, Ron Kramer, Willie Davis, Vince Lombardi, Paul Hornung, Max McGee, Henry Jordan, Jim Taylor, Jerry Kramer and yours truly.

I was the first of the inductees to speak that evening, and needless to say, I was extremely nervous. I stood up and praised my teammates, thanked the fans, and acknowledged Coach Lombardi's greatness. I introduced my father-in-law, my mother-in-law, and all of my children. I felt pretty good when I sat down.

Paul Hornung was next up. He began by saying, "I think Fuzzy forgot someone. I'd like to introduce you to his wife, Sue." There was great laughter, and Paul had a terrific way of smoothing it over, but I still felt like crawling under the table. I was glad Paul was paying attention, and that he was the next to speak, or Sue may never have forgiven me.

The guys were all dressed up in suits and ties, the gals were in evening gowns, and it was quite a ceremony. We won five World Championships and two Super Bowls together. To have that many teammates that were All-Pro and to be inducted into the Packers Hall of Fame together was very, very special.

Bart Starr and Fuzzy.

My induction into the Wisconsin Athletic Hall of Fame in 2003 was rewarding for many reasons. First, I'm a Wisconsin boy. My dream as a boy growing up in Altoona was to play basketball at Wisconsin. I didn't dream about playing football at Wisconsin, only because I never played football in high school. To be inducted into the Wisconsin Athletic Hall of Fame exceeded my boyhood dreams.

I was actually inducted into the Indiana Football Hall of Fame before the Wisconsin Hall of Fame. Walt Reiner, my coach at Valparaiso University, was with me to accept the award in Indianapolis. I was also inducted into Valparaiso's Athletics Hall of Fame. I will always have a special place in my heart for my coaches and teammates at Valparaiso University.

In the early 90's, Coach Mike Holmgren had me address the team before the Chicago Bears game. The players were enthusiastic and interested in hearing about the Bears-Packers rivalry through the years. I told them how important it was to beat the Bears. I had their attention and thought I did a good job. When I finished, they gave me a standing ovation. I shook every player's hand. That was the end of my career as a motivational speaker. We LOST the next day!

In 1993, then Packers General Manager Ron Wolf decided to bring back former Packers stars to serve as honorary captains. I was invited back on December 26, 1993 for the game against the Los Angeles Raiders. It had been almost 26 years since I had been part of the team, so I was very excited. It was an extremely cold day, not unlike the Ice Bowl. I was honored to represent the Packers alongside the other captains at mid-field for the coin toss. The Packers beat the Raiders 28-0. Naturally, I inspired the team to victory!

Fuzzy returns to Lambeau Field as Honorary Captain. He is seen here on the sidelines with the Packers preparing for the coin toss.

Individually, my most satisfying award was being voted All-Pro in 1962, receiving the most votes of ANY player – period! That still amazes me and makes me proud. After all the years I struggled to get into the league, I not only proved that I could play, but I proved that I was as good at that position as anyone in the league. That was a great award. I was voted to the All-Pro Team three times during my career. In my opinion, I played the guard position as well as anyone that ever played it. I know it may seem a little cocky to say, but that's the way I feel. Sue smiles when she hears me talk like that.

There's nothing wrong with taking pride in a job well done. It's part of what Coach Lombardi tried to instill in his players. It doesn't mean you're arrogant. It means you care, and I cared a great deal about the way I played and the way I was perceived by those that truly understood the

game. Don't get me wrong, I cared about what the fans thought. But, I cared more about the opinions of the men in the locker room, my teammates and coaches.

Golf is one of my favorite retirement activities. I don't take nearly as much pride in my performance on the golf course, though. I used to play at least three days a week during the winter when we had our place in Naples, Florida. Now, I don't play golf in the winter, but more than make up for it during the beautiful Wisconsin summers.

Fuzzy's 63 Bar hosts three golf tournaments each year in May, July and September. I also play in a number of charity golf outings to benefit cancer, Children's Hospital, diabetes and other worthwhile causes. I believe in giving back to the community. The most notable outings are the Vince Lombardi Classic, Packers Hall of Fame Golf Outing and the Ray Nitschke Players Classic.

I used to travel to Detroit, Milwaukee, St. Louis and College Station, Texas, to play in various charity golf tournaments. I've slowed down and now limit my participation to local events, with one exception. I attend the annual Fuzzy Thurston Open in Elkhart, Indiana. The event consists of local Packers fans that raise money for charity.

I've got a 32 handicap. That's legit. The best round of my life was breaking 80, once, with a 77 at Antigo Bass Lake Country Club. That's not too good for a player that used to be on the Altoona High School Golf Team. I joke and tell people that my game would be better if I didn't have to work all winter. Like I said, we used to have a place in Naples, but now we rent a condominium in Fort Myers Beach.

Our son, Griff, has a store on the pier of Fort Myers Beach and lives in an apartment on the beach. He operates a business that rents out beach chairs and umbrellas, and they're green and gold, naturally. He also has

Fuzzy and Sue enjoying time with their grandchildren Freddy and Olivia

a little store beneath his apartment, and three kiosks, selling bait and souvenirs, tourist stuff.

When I go there, I help rent the chairs and the umbrellas, which means I'm visiting with Packers fans from all over the country. It's a beautiful beach, and the tourists treat me great. It's good work if you can get it.

While I'm hawking chairs and umbrellas, Sue's either doing crossword puzzles or taking part in her other favorite hobby: Talking to our daughter, Tori, by telephone. Tori and Sue talk every day, and I mean every day, just like Sue and her mother did. I guess it's an Eggleston tradition. Naturally, our three children are a very important part of our retirement.

Mark, our oldest, was born May 8, 1958, in San Antonio while I was in the Army. He was only a few months old when we came to Wisconsin. Mark was very well traveled before he was a year old. I played for the Bears, the Eagles a second time, and then it was off to Winnipeg, Canada.

He has always taken a great interest in sports. Perhaps it began when I took him to St. Norbert College one day during training camp. I wanted my son to see where Dad ate, slept and studied during the six weeks he was away at training camp.

We were in the hallway of the dormitory, and we ran into Coach Lombardi. Mark was probably four or five years old at the time, and I said, "Mark, tell Coach who your favorite team is."

Mark smiled, looked up and said, "The Chicago Bears."

I was embarrassed, until I looked at Coach Lombardi, who started laughing like hell. I started laughing along with him, while Mark just stood there wondering what was so funny.

A few years later, I told George Halas, Head Coach of the Chicago Bears, the story at a football banquet. A short time later, I received a note from him in which he wrote, "Dear Mark, you are right. Your Dad is the greatest guard. It was my mistake. Sincerely, George Halas." Of course, Halas was referring to the fact that he once traded me from the Bears to the Eagles. Unfortunately, we lost that valued note, or it would have appeared in this book. I still get a kick out of that story.

Mark was very strong willed as a boy. The morning of the Ice Bowl, I was in Green Bay getting ready for the game, and I called Sue to tell her and her parents and the kids to stay home. It was just too cold. Well, when Sue told Mark he had a fit. He said, "If my Dad's playing in the game, I'm going." Then he put on his snow clothes and started walking toward the highway. Sue's dad had to get in the car and go get him.

Sue ended up taking Mark to the game. They sat bundled up in sleeping bags and were actually pretty warm. Mark was fine, and he didn't dare complain to his mother about the cold after the fit he threw.

Sue and their son Mark arrive at the Ice Bowl.

When Mark returned to school after Christmas, he had to write a paper for one of his classes. He was only nine years old at the time and wrote a story about the furnace going out at our house and how cold he was. He mentioned staying at Max McGee's apartment with his girlfriend, which was probably shunned at the time. He never mentioned attending the Ice Bowl. We laugh now, but I'm sure that paper made us look like bad parents at the time.

Sue Thurston with son Mark.

Mark was always his younger brother Griff's biggest fan. Mark didn't play football because of a bad back. He could have been jealous of Griff's athletic success, but wasn't. Mark was a good athlete, too, though. We sponsored the Left Guard softball team for him and his friends for years. Sue and I and her parents went to all of his games. They were really good, too. Today, he is one of the managers at Fuzzy's 63 Bar and Grill.

Griff was born July 16, 1959, in Madison. The doctor induced labor so I could see Griff being born before I had to leave to Baltimore for the Colts' training camp. After Griff was born, I drove to Baltimore, was then immediately traded to Green Bay, and had to turn around and drive right back.

Griff is a very easygoing, laid-back person. He used to stay up with Sue and watch "The Tonight Show" and munch popcorn. When Johnny Carson died, he called his mother to let her know how bad he felt, and how much fun he had all those years watching Johnny Carson with her.

I never pushed the kids into sports. If they were interested, I would help them if they asked, and that was about it. Sue and I did go to all their games, though.

The Thurston kids all grown up. L to R: Mark, Tori and Griff.

Griff was a star running back at Neenah High School, and he played for the North All-Stars in the state's first high school all-star game in 50 years. He scored the first touchdown in the game. He received a football scholarship to Wisconsin, but he tore up his knee in spring practice. He played in the spring game, and had done well, too. When he called to say he was injured, it was one of those calls a parent hates to get. Griff transferred to Rochester Junior College in Minnesota, rehabilitated his knee and ended up having a very nice career there.

It's funny, but Sue never worried about whether I would be injured in a game. It was a whole different story with Griff. That was her son out there, and she worried about him constantly.

Tori, our baby girl, was born November 1, 1962. Victoria Sue Thurston was seven years old when she got her first horse, an American Saddle Bred named Lucky Prince. It was a Christmas gift. She had her ponytails and was wearing a red jacket, and we had the stall decorated for Christmas.

Sue and Fuzzy with their daughter Tori at a horse competition.

She began entering show horse competitions, and she won a lot of awards on her horse, Harvey. When she was thirteen, she took first place in the World Championship Horse Show in Louisville. We did a lot of traveling to see her compete in horse shows in those days. We went to Milwaukee, Madison, La Crosse, Janesville, Minneapolis and Northwestern University in Evanston, Illinois.

Tori competed in horse shows until she was a junior in high school. She was also a cheerleader at Neenah, and she went on to graduate from the University of Wisconsin-Stevens Point. Today, she works at Fuzzy's Tickets and Tours.

I'm so proud of my family. They were always there to love and support me, and still are. That makes my retirement special. I'm not sure what God has planned for the rest of my life, but I treat each day as special, because you never know when it may be your last. I plan to continue to enjoy my family, my friends, the Green Bay Packers and their wonderful fans until the day I die. For me, it has been and continues to be *A Wonderful World.*

Bill Wenzel

is Fuzzy Thurston's business partner and President of Fuzzy's Tickets and Tours. Bill is the founder and former President of the Official Tour Company of the Green Bay Packers. An innovator in the Packers tour business, Bill has provided Packers fans worldwide with ticket, tailgate and tour packages since 1986.

Douglas Golner

is a freelance grahic artist and designer based in Milwaukee WI, producing work for a variety of graphic design and web clients. Most recently he completed a project for Fuzzy Thurston's teammate Jerry Kramer's *Inside the The Locker Room, the Lost Lombardi Tapes from Super Bowl II* project, including CD packaging, book design and promotional collateral.

Contributor, **Chris Havel**

is the head sports columnist for the *Green Bay Press Gazette* and a sports radio talk show host. Chris has authored several books, including *FAVRE* – which climbed to #4 on the New York Times best-seller list.